Jochen Roef, Jozefien De Feyter & Carolien Boom

RIO

Less Contact

How to win buyers' trust in a turbulent digital world

More Impact

Lannoo
Campus

This book was originally published as
Mensen raken = klanten maken, LannooCampus, 2020

D/2020/45/502 – ISBN 978 94 014 7342 2 – NUR 802

COVER AND ILLUSTRATIONS   Soon
LAYOUT   Keppie & Keppie

© The authors & Lannoo Publishers nv, Tielt, 2020.

Uitgeverij LannooCampus is part of Lannoo Uitgeverij,
the book and multimedia division of Uitgeverij Lannoo nv.

LannooCampus Publishers
Vaartkom 41 bus 01.02   Postbus 23202
3000 Leuven   1100 DS Amsterdam
Belgium   The Netherlands
WWW.LANNOOCAMPUS.COM

Contents

Foreword

————

By Pieterjan Bouten, CEO Showpad

As founder and CEO of Showpad, I have spent a great deal of time in recent years with the vendors and leaders of many of the world's most successful companies. From large multinationals such as Johnson & Johnson, Coca-Cola and Atlas Copco to successful family businesses and SMEs.

There is one constant that unites successful companies today. They have realized that it is no longer just about the best product or the sharpest price, and instead fully commit to the sales experience. It is the vision of Showpad and the authors of this book that the sales experience is the ultimate differentiator.

A few years ago, an analyst from a reputable research agency wrote a blogpost entitled 'The Death of the Salesperson'. This blogpost initiated a remarkably interesting debate about the future of the sales professional.

At a time when the Amazons of this world reign, and automation and artificial intelligence are the new normal, there are many voices emerging that question the future of the salesperson. To the point that some people are convinced that algorithms and bots will eventually render the role of the salesperson superfluous.

Technological advancements have given today's customer superpowers. They are better informed and have higher expectations. They have all the information they need – literally – at their fingertips and have become much more articulate. The days of the classic salesman whose focus is exclusively on price, product and, with the help of classic sales techniques, 'forcing' the customer into a decision are numbered.

Few people enjoy having a product or service forced onto them. However, people do like to buy products and services. Nobody wants to be sold to, yet most people like to buy. The big shift in sales is that nowadays the customer and his needs are central. This offers incredible opportunities for all organizations to create value. It also ensures that everyone who comes into contact with customers in their role can have a much greater impact and bring a much more valuable interpretation to a commercial function.

For most companies, the human factor will continue to be decisive in achieving that sales experience. That is where RIO as a model offers added value. I do not believe that algorithms, bots and automation will take over everything. On the contrary: it is only people who can really listen, surprise and bring that extra bit of magic into the sales process.

Technology will play an increasingly important role in ensuring that salespeople are better informed and that they can be coached. That is a good thing, because the role of the salesperson will not only become broader and more interesting, but also much more challenging.

Putting the customer first also means investing in your people. Sales training and coaching, as well as a better understanding of the sales process, all play an incredibly important role in this. That is why this book is such a pleasure to read. The RIO model is based on the human model. It provides insight into the undercurrent of commercial interactions and transactions. It clarifies the experience customers are looking for as individuals. The many practical examples and stories from the field are also enriching.

So, the salesperson is far from dead. Long may he live!

Introduction

———

We are living in special times. Both the commercial profession and our planet have come under pressure. If we do not change catastrophe lurks around the corner.

Are you wondering what these subjects have to do with each other? On the surface, nothing; in essence, everything. A book today that only talks about 'selling more' is no longer relevant. 'Selling more' of what? 'Selling more' to whom? Selling more worthless stuff to people who do not need it?

It is time for a paradigm shift: in this book, we call it 'RIO-integrated selling'.

RIO-integrated selling is based on two or more businesspeople meeting each other with conscious intention. Two parties who use their heads, hearts and guts to trade products and services that are worthwhile, not only for the direct stakeholders, but also for the greater good.

'Becoming a great sales person,
implies becoming a great person.'

Our promise to you is ambitious: integrate the knowledge from this book and you will become a richer person, not only materially but intrinsically. Not only will your revenue increase, but also your self-esteem and the positive influence on the people around you.

Bold statement? You bet! But we're going for shared responsibility here. We're providing you with a book full of practical tips, valuable insights and far-reaching inspiration. What we ask of you is a close reading and daily application. The full impact of RIO will only show itself after integration into your knowing, feeling and acting.

Customer typology is nothing new. There are many psychological models that offer insight into how customers think and how to deal with them. But this book goes a step further than that. Typology is the starting point for a deeper connection with the customer and yourself. Because what is the use of pretending to have the same hobbies as our customer if he can check our Facebook? What good will come from imitating the style of the customer when the true quality of our product can be read online?

We are entering the age of true sales. Of genuine connection. Connection creates energy; there is nothing woolly about it. Real connection shines a light on the true concerns of the organization, society and the planet. With a global 'army' of 21 million salespeople, companies have the ability to generate a positive impact like no other. The time is ripe for organizations that create valuable products and for sales professionals who bring them to their customers with pure intentions.

You can see RIO as a behavioral method, however, this book is not a manual for actors. 'Fake it until you make it' is a thing of the past. RIO is a sincere invitation to look at yourself in relation to your customer and to grow as a person and a professional.

Are you ready to make a difference? *Join us #wearerio!*

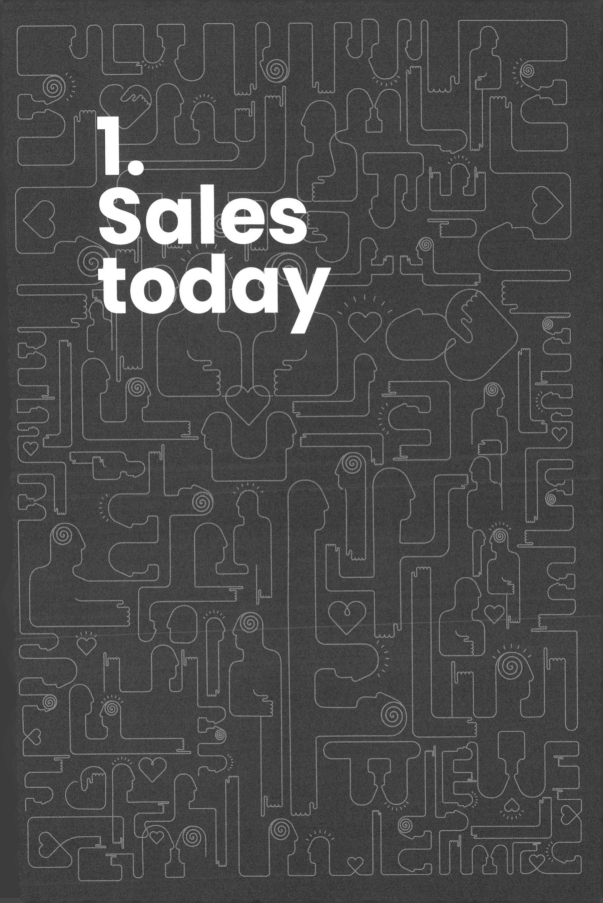

1.
Sales
today

*What makes
sales different today
than before?*

——

*What are crucial skills
for the modern
salesperson?*

——

*What added value
does RIO have for the
modern salesperson
and marketer?*

Will there still be salespeople in 2030? Opinions are divided. Believers say that the mix of empathy, know-how and solution-orientation will always give people a head start on machines. Non-believers predict that artificially intelligent chatbots will take over the conversation with customers and drones will be delivering products ordered online to our homes, day and night.

No one knows who will be right. What is certain, however, is that human salespeople have to develop themselves because the sales profession is evolving. The more than 50,000 sales-related books on Amazon are a case in point. Yet the profession has only made a handful of growth spurts throughout history and only recently undergone a radical shift. We have now reached a point of no return. What follows is a quick sketch of the evolution of sales, as well as an interpretation of what makes sales in 2020 fundamentally different than before.

Pitching USPs: unique selling points

Before the 1970s, sales was straightforward. Whoever exhibited his product most convincingly won the customer over. Sellers went from door to door armed with suitcases full of pots, pans, perfumes, shoes and lingerie. Even less obvious products such as telephones, coffins, Persian carpets, pool tables and swimming pools were dragged around the country in miniature.

During this period, vendors were drilled on how to energetically pitch to customers, cleverly devising storylines with the aim of convincing them of an *offer they couldn't refuse*. The scripts were produced behind closed doors and were full of USPs, unique selling points, or the product's most impressive features. The purpose of the sales pitch was to unobtrusively drive the customer into a corner that he would be unable to leave unless he continued buying. Storylines played on pain and pleasure, while a highly sophisticated carrot-and-stick strategy would cause the 'dazed' prospect to crack under so much sales violence. During this period, sellers were masters in overcoming objections and employed a wide range of *closing techniques*. The well-known expression 'always be closing' dates from this period.

What did the salesperson look like in the USP era? Characteristic of top sellers was an outspoken winner's mentality. Resilience, perseverance and flexibility were indispensable qualities. In order to succeed you had to be a powerhouse that could arouse enough sympathy to get in past the front door. Moreover, the salesperson had to have a 'thick skin', and 'selective hearing' came in handy, given that the intention was to tell the rehearsed story despite the prospect's resistance.

Nowadays this form of sales is called 'transactional' and it occurs sporadically in sectors where the customer and the seller only have one sales conversation. Sectors that sell by phone typically use more scripts and sales pitches, with *The Wolf of Wall Street* as the best-known cinematic example.

Discovering UBRs: unique buying reasons

Mack Hanan's 1970 book *Consultative Selling* was to sales what Elvis was to music: a swinging alternative to the way things were done at the time. For the first time ever, the focus was not on the salesman's product or service, but on the customer and his needs. Top salespeople acted as consultants who delved into the customer's challenges before offering a solution.

In this period the term UBR was born, unique buying reasons. From then on, the customer's situation was the focus, and the sales professional would search for the unique reasons the prospect should buy the product or service. UBRs consisted of two categories: problems the customer had to solve and ambitions he wanted to realize. The sales professional's first objective was to discover the customer's needs and desires through thoughtful questioning. The next step was a bespoke product presentation. For the first time in sales, the product was 'king' and the product's specific fit 'emperor'! Customers no longer wanted generic presentations of the product's features; they wanted the specific benefits with regards to their needs and ambitions.

The shift from product sales to consultative sales would result in a huge about-turn in sales professionals' skills. Perhaps the biggest change was the leap from 80% speaking to 80% listening. Consultative sales was a dialogue with the customer that sought to apply the principle 'first seek to under-stand, then to be understood'. From now on, salespeople were expected to be 'gentlemen and gentlewomen' who gallantly put the customer first. Never-theless, relinquishing the control that a script offered proved to be a struggle for product sellers during retraining. After all, that control had been the key to success in the previous era. Asking open-ended questions meant opening the door to unwanted answers that reduced the chance of success, a risk the *hard seller* was unwilling to take. From now on, the consultative seller would seek the richness of unfiltered customer information, which he then gratefully used to create a bespoke presentation. In consultative selling, testosterone gave way to listening skills, domination to dialogue. Vendors were still trained in overcoming objections, but these became less common as a result of the now highly relevant argumentation.

Consultative selling in its derivative forms (*SPIN selling, solution selling, customer-centric selling, insight selling,* etc.) is still the most widely used sales methodology in value-added contexts. Modern sales organizations such as Showpad further facilitate their sales team's consultative sales process with:

» ICPs (Ideal Customer Profiles): The profiles of 'ideal customers', who are targeted as prospects.
» Persona: A detailed character description of the targeted contact person. Who is this person? What interests him? How does he make decisions?
» Sector trends: Developments that influence companies in specific sectors and serve as a starting point for commercial discussions.
» 'Use cases': Reference projects from certain sectors in which the original need and delivered solution are described. These are used as guidelines during the sales process with similar customers.
» 'Customer journeys': Road maps detailing the process that the customer goes through with his needs and how the sales rep can respond to them.

The targeted use of this documentation, often brought together in a 'sales playbook', enables consultative salespeople to both look for pain points with their prospect and maintain control of the conversation. This advanced variant of consultative sales is known as 'guided selling'.

Offering UDEs: unique desired experiences

And that brings us to today. How different are today's sales and what are the gamechangers that modern sales professionals must take into account?

——

KNOWLEDGE IS POWER

Constant connectivity has irrevocably rearranged the power relationship between buyer and seller. Whereas the seller used to derive part of his right to speak from product knowledge, the buyer now no longer needs the sales professional in order to be informed. The figures do not lie. Research by Gartner has shown that the modern buyer now spends only 17% of his time meeting potential suppliers, while investing three times as much time (45%) in reading independent reviews. As a result, the average prospect will have completed 57% of his buying process before meeting a sales professional.

HYPER-PERSONALIZATION AND CO-CREATION

The time when everyone could buy a Ford in the color of their choice, as long as it was black (Henry Ford's statement in 1909), is long gone. Advertising leaflets are composed on the basis of recent purchases, cola cans are printed with first names, text messages come to life with a personal emoji, and algorithms determine which film will be playing tonight. Buyers can be as authentic as they desire, while sales and marketing respond by analyzing millions of bytes of behavioral data to make the right offer at the right moment. If the desired product does not yet exist, it will be developed with the customer. Standard products are out, co-creation is in!

HYPER-CONVENIENCE

Today, more than ever, the customer is being pampered. Orders placed before 11:59 PM will be delivered the next day to the address of your choice. For a few euros extra, delivery can be made the same day, even on Sunday if necessary. The customer does not have to bother searching because global giants like Amazon and Alibaba have made sure that everything can be found under one roof. The one-stop shop DELUXE. Can you imagine a customer having to visit two webshops? We are becoming lazy buyers and *we like it a lot*!

With their own *hyper-convenience* concepts, the following companies have understood that the modern customer has neither time nor energy to lose:

» Partena Health Insurance Fund makes use of an online counter. As a client, you no longer have to physically go to the office to submit doctor's notes. You simply scan them in via your smartphone and a refund is automatically made to your account.

» The British laundry service Dropwash picks up baskets of dirty laundry at home and delivers them back, washed and ironed, within two days. Payment is done via a PayPal account.

» Who Gives A Crap delivers packages of high-quality toilet paper made from bamboo fibers to your home so that you will never run out of it again.

» Dollar Shave Club does the same with razor blades and was recently sold to Unilever for 1 billion (!) dollars.

HYPER-COMPLEXITY

In stark contrast to the ease of use and tailored products stands the increased complexity of the purchase decision. The main culprit: choice overload. Both private and professional purchasers are being bombarded with an endless flow of information whose truthfulness varies between fake news and sincere user reviews. Everyone knows that the internet can be manipulated, and that the new generation of scammers are online. Who or what can be trusted becomes the key question. There is now a great need for reliable guides to accompany the buyer through this treacherous jungle.

THE IMPULSE TO SHARE

In the midst of hyper-connectivity, a phenomenon has arisen with an enormous impact on the way we influence and are influenced during the purchase process: the impulse to share. This trend has different origins. More than ever before, we now have the opportunity as individuals to make our unique mark. The impact of a bad review can be huge, which means that we, as affected customers, are suddenly taken seriously.

A second important reason for sharing appears to be the desire to improve the lives of others. When a fundamental need is not met during the purchase, the buyer wants to spare others this experience and sends out a warning.

The influence of the 'sharing impulse' on commercial interactions cannot be overestimated. The popularity of professional peer-review websites such as G2Crowd, which will soon exceed 1 million reviews, proves that the seller is by no means the only source of information that the modern prospect turns to.

Unique desired experience

The traditional customer relationship has been turned upside down. Research shows that customers expect ever shorter, but nevertheless deeper, contacts. Furthermore, customers demand that the vendor remain involved in the long term, at least until the solution is implemented and the impact visible. Where the sales rep used to close the door after the transaction, he is now responsible for the effectiveness of the solution and the customer's feelings about it.

Now, customers want a unique purchasing experience that goes beyond price, quality and product features in the decision-making process. For sellers, it is impossible to simply promise and not deliver. If they do, reality will overtake them through customer reviews.

Today, sales professionals no longer sell products, but a total experience or a *unique desired experience*. This experience is personal, tailored and effortless. The selling organization offers added value during every step of the process. The customer is king and expects generous treatment. When everything is finished, he will let the world know whether it was good or not.

Every crisis is an opportunity

The facts are what they are, digitalization and hyper-personalization are here to stay. Selling will never be what it used to be and neither panic nor nostalgia is going to help us. The key questions become: Where is the opportunity in this seemingly hopeless situation? How can the modern sales professional remain standing in an era of relentless change? What are the skills that make the difference and create undeniable value?

Guides

In a recent Gartner study, 77% of B2B buyers indicated that their last purchase decision was extremely complex. As difficult as selling has become in 2020, the purchasing process has become even more complex, says Gartner's VP Advisory, Brent Adamson.[1]

First of all, customers need to get a clear picture of their needs and requirements. Some are visible and others hidden. Then the buyer has to work his way through an unlimited number of information sources in order to arrive at a list of potential suppliers. Discussions with these suppliers, who usually promote their product unilaterally, should lead to a list of clear pros and cons that can be weighed against each other to come to the right decision. Then, internal stakeholders must be informed, consulted and convinced and the return on investment must be tangible in order to free up a budget. After the negotiation and purchase, the solution has to be implemented, which often means selling internally to a colleague who is not expecting change. Continuous follow-up at the end of the journey will ensure whether the anticipated added value is realized or not.

Looking at this process, we might almost feel sorry for the buyer. It is clear that the customer needs a reliable partner who knows the concerns and challenges at every stage and provides targeted support. This is the only way for the salesperson to assure his customer that he will get through the purchase process in one piece.

Challenging and offering perspectives

Recent sales methodologies such as *challenger sales* and *RAIN selling* argue that sellers need to excel in two competences: challenging customers and offering a positive perspective. Just as a doctor protects his patient from internet diagnoses and self-medication, a sales rep should vigorously remind his customer of the dangers of online information and poor business choices. The sales professional bases his statements on business acumen: research and know-how based on the market. Additionally, practical examples, use cases, references and testimonials offer the customer the necessary positive perspective to take a step forward. Being able to respectfully yet vigorously challenge the customer to look at his situation from a broader perspective is a crucial competence for modern sales professionals.

Co-creation through 'design thinking'

In their recent book *From Selling to Co-Creating*, authors Régis Lemmens, Bill Donaldson and Javier Marcos develop the argument that standard products and services in B2B sales are a thing of the past. Each business customer's context is so specific that seller and customer are now obliged to co-create a unique product as part of a long-term partnership. The customer brings in the knowledge of his company; the vendor of his product, market and his technical know-how.

According to *Forbes* magazine, co-creation, the process in which customer-oriented innovation is central, goes hand in hand with *design thinking*, a methodology used in creative product development. Through a thorough needs analysis, a clear problem definition is achieved. This is then followed by an *ideation phase* in which out-of-the-box solutions are encouraged. After selecting the most valuable idea, a prototype is built and tested.

It should be clear that in the co-creative sales process the customer makes an active contribution and becomes co-responsible for the end result. Customer and seller are equal partners. This situation then calls for two new sales competences:

1 Convincing the customer to take an active role.
2 Giving the customer the space to actively contribute (read: forfeiting absolute control over the sales process and the predicted outcome!).

Working with technology

In the age of digital customer convenience, the sales professional is not alone in his task of convincing the prospect. The customer experience is much broader than the 17% face-to-face contact that the average customer still has with their salesperson. More than ever before, the statement 'put a good sales rep in a bad system and the system wins every time' applies.

The seller is now part of a complete ecosystem of marketing and sales tools that all function to initiate the right experience at the right moment. Working with applications for geographic market analysis (Geotop), social selling (Sales Navigator), automatic prospecting (Hootsuite), interactive presentations (Showpad) and click-behavior-based follow-up (Salesflare) will become the new normal. Knowing how to employ *growth hacking technology* is then an essential skill.

Creating trust

In and amongst all of the frenzy and change, the primordial competence of all sales skills is once again undergoing an upgrade: inspiring customer confidence!

Research by HubSpot has shown that confidence in vendors is at an all-time low. In a recent study only 3% of all respondents said they trust sales professionals. Only politicians, stockbrokers, car dealers and lobbyists fared worse.

Both remarkable and crucial is that the impact of trust in sales is twofold:

a Of course, the salesperson has to create trust in his relationship with the customer. If there is no trust, there will be a reluctance to share, listen, process and accept information. Suspicion is the enemy of cooperation. It is not for nothing that CSO Insights, the research department of the Miller Heiman Group, designates the *trusted partner status* as the most constructive and profitable position a sales rep can acquire in the customer relationship.

b At the same time, a second type of trust also plays a crucial role in the modern purchasing process: the degree to which the salesperson can inspire self-confidence in his customer! You read that right: 'The degree to which the salesperson can influence the self-confidence of his customer!'

Purchasing has become extremely complex. The customer can fall prey to a crippling fear of failure and choose to avoid the decision altogether. The extent to which the seller is able to influence the customer's self-assurance determines the speed and constructiveness of the purchase decision. This coaching role is completely new in the curriculum of the modern salesperson.

Emotional intelligence 3.0

'Sales organizations shouldn't be solving a sales problem, they should be solving a human problem.'

– BRENT ADAMSON, VP GARTNER

Selling in 2020 is a challenge because purchasing has become extremely complex. Sales professionals need to inspire unprecedented levels of trust to be able to question, inform and challenge their potential customers. Equally, they need to be skilled in guiding, supporting and coaching their customer so as to facilitate the purchasing decision.

Ideally, customers will have a kind of 'best man' feeling when it comes to their salespeople: the person who knows and respects them, who is caring and wise and vigorously defends their interests with the conviction that only then can everyone win. Customers need to trust their salespeople blindly in order to be able to give them access to the confidential information and emotional considerations that surround the purchase decision.

All this requires an exceptional degree of emotional intelligence from salespeople, an ability to connect quickly and deeply and so motivate a prospect towards an active partnership. Salespeople must have a clear mind, an open heart and pure decisiveness in order to offer their clients the personalized experience they are looking for. These are all qualities that can be developed, which seamlessly brings us to the next chapter: RIO as a tool for acquiring razor-sharp insight into people. *Let's go!*

3   WHAT IS RIO?

The click

RIO is chemistry in sales. It is the flow that arises between two professionals and gets things moving. It is the click, the wavelength, the alignment, the similarity or one of the many other terms given to the event in which businesspeople open up to each other, believe that they can mean something to each other and in which exchange arises. There is an atmosphere of respect, safety and equality. It is the situation in which one does not have to convince the other, in which opinions do not clash, but instead both parties contribute insights to a solution that is valuable.

This chemistry, which every sales professional knows is crucial in sales, is no accident. It seems to arise randomly but, in reality, does not. The click is linked to the psychological mechanisms surrounding trust, because sales is about trust, whether it be rudimentary trading or in virtual bitcoin applications. The central question is always: 'Is this situation safe?' To eliminate the uncertainty factor, people scan the interaction in all its facets: the environment, the people, the circumstances. Exactly how this rapid screening takes place differs from person to person and is determined by the individual's RIO 'channel of trust'.

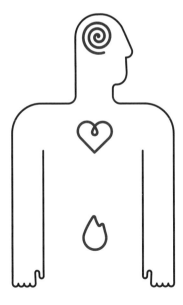

The RIO model describes three fundamentally different ways in which clients build trust and it shows the impact that this has on their thinking, feeling and acting. RIO offers the sales professional a concrete *roadmap* for meeting, informing and convincing the client within his or her world. In doing so, the model makes manageable one of the most uncontrollable aspects of sales: human diversity.

RIO begins with the observation that all people are equal in their innate resources to move through life. Every human being has a heart to feel, a head to think and a belly to convert food into energy. Although these three 'tools' are ideally deployed in a balanced way during life's events, we have nevertheless developed a preference across our evolution. Our preferred tool is our 'primary RIO channel', and we thrust this one forward during uncomfortable situations such as a sales conversation.

Three channels of trust

RELATIONAL CHANNEL OF TRUST

People with the relational channel are 'feelers'. They are gentle and tolerant people's people. Above all, they require approval and a sense of agreement. They are sensitive to others' needs, pick up on moods and connect in the group. Relational people are natural diplomats who do not want to shock or bruise. In their environment they are often known as the positive, sympathetic helper who prefers to avoid conflicts and is always ready to welcome others with a coffee, warm heart and listening ear. Relational people excel in 'human connection'.

INFORMATIVE CHANNEL OF TRUST

People with an informative channel of trust are 'thinkers'. They get their energy from studying information and structuring tasks. Informative people hate chaos, unprofessionalism and the expression of emotion. Informative people hold back in situations where they have no knowledge or skill. They need time to process information and stimuli. In their environment they are known as rational thinkers who are always prepared and masters at discovering 'inconsistencies', or data that is not 100% correct. Informative people excel in 'factual analysis'.

People with an outgoing channel of trust are 'doers'. They get their energy from tackling matters and generating impact. Outgoing people are extroverted and intense. They like to get things moving and get people to join them. They do not shy away from strong statements and conflicts. 'No shine without friction.' Outgoing people are fast and impulsive. Action is what drives them. That is why they want things to be simple and concrete. In their environment, they are known as the assertive troop drivers and truth challengers. Outgoing people excel in 'concrete action'.

Sales, trust and security

Every sales professional knows the feeling of a difficult sales conversation. Seller and customer talk past each other, arguments miss the mark, objections keep coming and both parties cling to their own point of view.

RIO reveals what is taking place 'in the undercurrent' of that moment and offers insight into awkward conversations from the perspective of trust. The model is highly relevant since research by HubSpot has shown that 97% of customers distrust sales professionals. In human psychology, a lack of trust equals a lack of security. That unsafe situation leads to different expectations and defense mechanisms in each of the three RIO customer types.

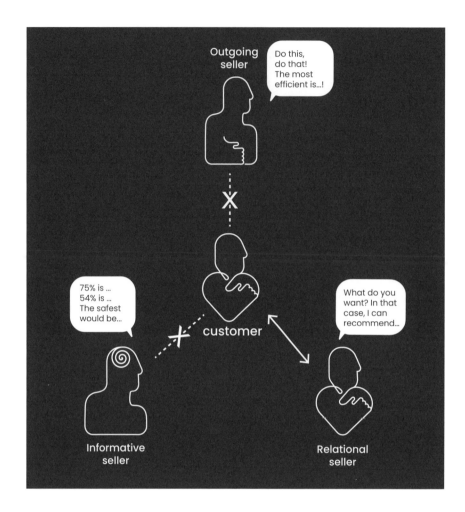

WHAT RELATIONAL CUSTOMERS EXPECT

Relational customers (RCs) gauge the sales situation according to people. They scan their interlocutor for sympathy and want to experience a sense of openness and warmth. They are looking for a partner who gives them personal attention, radiates patience and offers a tailored answer. For RCs, sincere friendliness means that people respect each other and have each other's best interests at heart. More than to the product itself, relational people are receptive to the salesperson and the pleasant atmosphere he creates. Visible signals of agreement and appreciation show the relational buyer that it is safe to open his channel of trust and interact freely. Conversely, an overly factual or action-oriented approach by the seller will lead the relational buyer to close his channel of trust. RCs decide with their hearts.

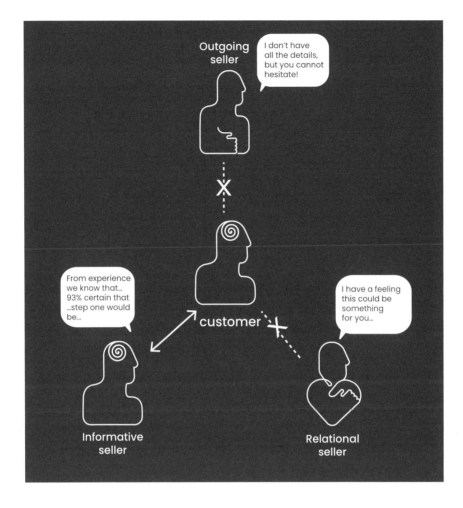

WHAT INFORMATIVE CUSTOMERS EXPECT

Informative customers (ICs) gauge the sales situation according to content. They scan their interlocutor for expertise and assess professionalism. They are looking for a professional who offers them information based on competence and experience. Background information, accreditations and certificates show them that the potential risks are covered by a discussion partner with know-how. ICs look for objective points of comparison on which to base their assessment. They do mathematical risk management and want to minimize the chance of a 'wrong' decision. Logic and structure equals control, which ensures that the informative customer opens up his channel of trust. On the other hand, unsubstantiated claims and instinctive estimations will lead to the informative customer's withdrawal. ICs decide with their heads.

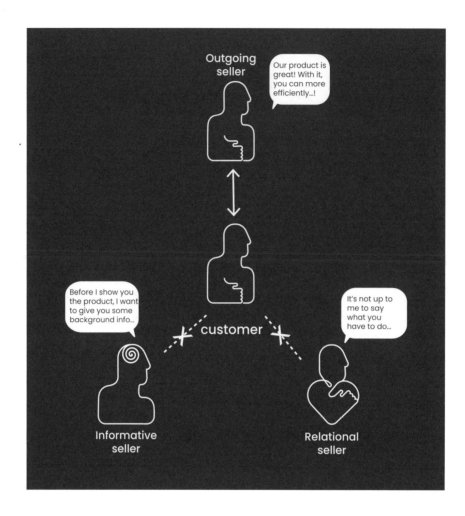

WHAT OUTGOING CUSTOMERS EXPECT

Outgoing customers (OCs) gauge the sales situation according to the energy. They scan their interlocutor for dynamism, passion and charisma. OCs want to see firmness and strength. In their view, weakness and doubt are a recipe for failure. Outgoing customers are looking for solutions that are efficient and effective and salespeople who fully believe in their product. They want to have their socks knocked off by spectacular benefits and predictable profits. They want to make instant progress, because standing still is going backwards. These people think fast and trust their intuition. They appraise potential suppliers within a fraction of a second. Demonstrated charisma unlocks their channel of trust, while softness and dullness put OCs to sleep. OCs decide with their gut.

Where does RIO come from?

We often get the feedback that as a model RIO is easy to understand and apply. This is not illogical, since RIO comes from people. Everyone has a head, a heart and a gut. Since ancient times, people have been fascinated by these 'centers' within our bodies and their connection with human psychology; however, it is recent neurological research that has finally led to a break-through. We will now share a concise overview of RIO's origins in different areas of knowledge.

Industry

The RIO model originated in the place where it is best applied: client conver-sations. As experienced experts in sales and sales coaching, we have wit-nessed hundreds of commercial conversations over the past 10 years in which the alignment with the customer often went wrong. Among other things, these resulted in the humorous anecdotes retold in this book. The RIO model, therefore, is the end product of studying the literature on the psychology of trust, combined with the determination to create a practical framework for our coaches. The three channels of trust have since passed the practical test and the model has been enhanced over the years with candid input from thousands of trainees who have followed our courses.

Neuroscience

Modern neurological research has shown that in addition to the brain cells in our heads, similar neural networks can be found around the heart and be-tween the intestines.[2] These cells, called neurons, are connected by branches called dendrites. As in the brain, these cells transmit signals to each other via neurotransmitters and join together in the nerve nodes that run along the spine.

What makes neural networks special is that they receive, process and store information separately from the brain. This happens locally in the body, and from there the signals are transmitted to the brain via the vagus nerve. There are 100 million neural 'brain' cells present in the intestines, which is the equivalent of a cat's brain. Around the heart there are 40,000.

Although the head, heart and abdominal brains have similar characteristics, they are not identical. Each neural network has its own function, subjects and language.

» The head brain is responsible for human thinking, or cognitive and analytical skills. In order to communicate with the head brain, we use logic and language. Everyone is familiar with the little voice in our head that never fails to offer 'advice' when making decisions in our lives.

» The heart brain, in turn, is responsible for human feeling, creating connection and living through values. Communication with the heart brain occurs through emotion and the wide range of human sentiments (joy, sadness, passion, disappointment, etc.).

» The abdominal brain has the function of body awareness, self-protection and action. Exchanging messages with the abdominal brain takes place via body sensations and sensory information. Just think of statements such as 'smelling fear', 'a bad feeling in my gut' and 'palpable tension'.

The most important added value of this research concerns the bridge that the neural networks provide between a physical place in the body and the psychological sensations that accompany it. The RIO channels of trust are given an identifiable place within the body, namely the heart (R), head (I) and gut (O), which is unique for a psychological model. This offers the advantage that we can directly influence how these three channels function through physical exercises. That promotes personal growth, which is the subject of the penultimate chapter of this book.

Human psychology

In 2012, we made use of the enneagram as basis for *Het Salesboek, voor elk type verkoper (The Sales Book, for every type of salesperson)*, employing the psychological drivers behind the various sales types as a springboard for increased commercial success. Although the enneagram is extremely valuable for stimulating self-development, it cannot describe the interaction between customer and salesperson. However, the basis of the nine drivers, which are the three centers of intelligence, lend themselves to this perfectly.

It was a Tuesday morning in Paris when 15 garage owners from a well-known car brand entered the room and we decided against working with the nine drivers of the enneagram. Instead, we explained the customer relationship through the three centers. RIO 1.0 was born!

Ancient philosophical traditions

Buddhism is one of the best-known philosophical traditions; it can essentially be described as follows: ending the suffering that comes with desiring things we do not have and having things we do not want. We simply have to sit, breathe, and maintain the clarity in our hearts and minds that we are part of a circle of compassion that unites us all.[3]

It is easy to identify the head, heart and gut in a definition that discusses a clear mind, a pure heart and peace in the abdominal center. It may reassure the reader of this book to recognize the link between RIO and a 2,500-year-old philosophical tradition that is more relevant today than ever and provides the basis of many professional and personal mindfulness programs

RIO in sales

At this point, it is interesting to look back at the first chapter of this book and point out the connection between the three eras in sales and RIO.

USP sales, in which customers were convinced with vigor of the advantages of the product, were undeniably based on outgoing dynamics. UBR sales, in which systematic questioning and thorough insight into the customer's situation led to detailed sales presentations, added the informative component to the sales profession. Finally, UDE sales, in which the personal experience of the customer took center stage, added a solid dose of relational dynamics.

In order to be successful in sales today, combining relational, informative and outgoing skills offers the only guarantee for exceeding customer expectations. Modern salespeople must possess a clear mind, receptive heart and pure purpose to provide the customer with a positive *buying experience*. Developing RIO sales skills is a must!

Developing and implementing RIO sales competences in an organization is a process. On an individual level, it starts with knowledge of the trust channels and the ability to notice them in interactions with customers. At the same time, sales professionals have to think about their own actions and become aware of their relationship with different customer types. As a final step, sales professionals develop complementary competences, skills that complement their established behavioral patterns. In this last step, frequent support is needed from the manager, colleagues and a coach. RIO should ideally be implemented as a common language within the organization, while the marketing materials, sales documentation, coaching tools and customer data in the CRM should be aligned with RIO. In this way, RIO not only becomes a nice model, but also a strategic choice that lifts the entire sales organization to a higher level of *customer-differentiated sales*.

The question then arises: Why would an organization invest in a RIO transformation process? What is the profit in the short and medium term? What is the impact on other departments? We will describe RIO's link with revenue growth, position-filling, sales training and coaching, internal communication and the choice of a sales methodology. So as to make everything concrete, real cases of progressive sales organization will be the recurring theme in this chapter.

Generating more revenue

Let's get straight to it: How does RIO increase revenue and margin? A metaphor will make things clear. The RIO channels of trust can be thought of as three languages utterly different in vocabulary, grammar and sentence structure. Keeping with the example, a buyer can speak English, Russian or Chinese. Although most sales professionals realize that customers vary, they underestimate the impact of this 'language difference'. Buyers with different RIO profiles think, feel and behave in fundamentally different ways. Not paying attention to the customer's preference is like having a sales conversation in English with a Chinese buyer.

EXAMPLE – LOSING A TOP PROSPECT

A temp consultant has managed to get an appointment with a renowned faucet manufacturer. When she is welcomed on-site by the person in charge of the purchase, she approaches him with a smile from ear to ear. He gives her a business-like handshake, combined with a severe facial expression. Determined to break the ice, she starts with a compliment shower about the building. The man listens impassively as they walk to his desk. Seated, he immediately proceeds to the business at hand without offering her anything to drink. The buyer wants to quickly assess whether this conversation will be interesting or not. The first question he asks is: 'Can you tell me what you know about our company?' The consultant sees her chance to boost the mood and gets excited: 'Well, my boyfriend and I are renovating our place at the moment and we were at Brico's this weekend. We were looking at your faucets and I have to say: they are just stunning. I think we're going to buy them!' Hopeful, she waits for an affirmative response that never comes. What instead follows is the question: 'Are you saying that you haven't analyzed our website?' Too surprised to improvise, she confesses: 'No, I haven't done that yet.' After which the buyer concludes: 'I think we'd better finish the conversation here.' Disillusioned, the consultant gets up and leaves the room after a formal farewell. Losing a top prospect as the result of a pronounced relational-informative mismatch can be painful..

EXAMPLE – DRESSED TO THE NINES

An outgoing salesperson has an important first interview with a prospective client at a national publisher. He is dressed to the nines: nice watch, shiny shoes and coiffed hair. After all, you do not get a second chance to make a first impression! With conviction and a preconceived objective, he swiftly approaches the receptionist. With a broad smile and a quick compliment, he asks after his contact person. Although the lady offers him a seat, he prefers to stand; his dynamic attitude radiates self-confidence. A business-like woman walks up and looks at the salesman inquisitively. He rushes toward her at a trot and enthusiastically grabs her outstretched hand. Weak handshake, he thinks. He tells the lady that she looks radiant today! She looks dubious, thanks him politely and invites him to enter her office. He walks along with her. After they have taken their seats, the salesman takes a few business cards and leaflets out of his bag. He opens the conversation: '*Voilà!* First of all, thank you for letting me come by. I'm convinced that our services could have a huge added value for your company! How many of you work here?'

The customer clearly needs a little more context and does not want to give herself away too quickly. She opens her laptop, which raises a wall between her and the seller. She announces that she would like to take notes during the conversation and keeps her eyes focused largely on her screen. 'Maybe you can tell me a little more about your company first? And about your background?'

The seller replies: 'As you know, I am the AM of company x; we specialize in ATS systems, and we currently offer the most efficient system on the market! That's why I'd love to hear what problems you're having at the moment.'

The HR manager explains that it is extremely important to be able to follow up with her people and that they are thinking in the long term about automating and optimizing various processes. They are currently doing a comparative study with different suppliers and are looking for an expert who can make smart analyses of current processes and assist them with the transformation.

The salesman starts to become impatient and says their system can do it all! In his enthusiasm he asks: 'How can I convince you to work with us?!'

The lady replies: 'Feel free to leave all your information and details, we'll look into it and contact you again.'

Although the outgoing seller felt that he had completely convinced the informative HR-manager, she never responds when he follows up...

It is evident that sales professionals who are proficient in the three RIO languages reach far more customers than those who only speak their 'native language'. Spontaneous statements resonate with one-third of the market, while the remaining two-thirds go hungry. RIO's leverage in sales growth is therefore huge.

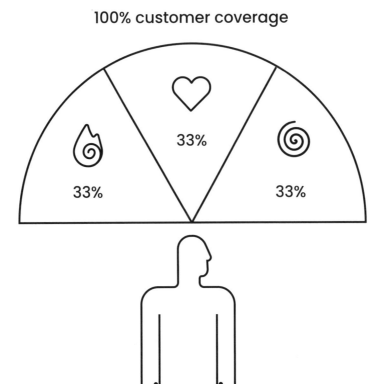

100% customer coverage

RIO salesperson

CUSTOMER CASE: PARTENA HEALTH INSURANCE FUND

Koen Vandendriessche, commercial manager at Partena Health Insurance Fund, discusses how they invested in the RIO methodology and saw their sales results and NPS scores improve rapidly. Koen is an enthusiastic, people-focused sales manager with a passion for the digitalization and optimization of processes that make things as easy as possible for his people.

Koen Vandendriessche: 'Two years ago, we started with a RIO test to map out our human capital. We wanted to know who had the most sales potential to stimulate proactivity in the organization. The goal was to distinguish the hunters from the farmers so that we could let everyone function based on their strengths. At Blinc Sales Institute they told us that there is a good salesperson hiding in everyone. So, with that "everybody has commercial talent" in hand, we went to work. We used the results to tell the service staff which sales profile they had. One has more of an informative way of selling and approaches a customer/prospect with figures and analyses. Others do this in an outgoing way, with strong words and decisiveness. We emphasize that every style is equally valuable. In that way we've actually ensured that the concepts hit home. Our people understand what their channel of trust is and that they, too, can be commercial. During the training courses, they're presented with techniques and answers for each RIO type. So, it's no longer "that's the way to do it" but instead there is a range and thus an opportunity to choose. The "hunger for sales" then comes automatically. Because it's tailored to their personality.'

CUSTOMER CASE: SYNERGY

Synergy is an HR partner whose business is arranging work for other people. They are focused on long-term, sustainable relationships with their customers. The reason they implemented RIO was because they were searching for a methodology that was in line with their corporate DNA, allowing people to remain themselves as well as soft sellers. Katy Lauwaert is a senior sales coach who always wants to get the best out of her trainees and found, in RIO, the missing key to working with them in a personalized manner.

Katy Lauwaert: 'I've been in the temping sector for 30 years and I've been given a lot of sales frameworks over the years. However, they never left me feeling completely satisfied because I'm convinced that connecting with a conversation partner is a very important asset in sales. When I became acquainted with RIO, I thought: "Of course, that's what I've been doing for years, only now it's substantiated and in a theoretical form!" For me, it was an eye-opener and a reassurance that we could achieve improved commercial results with confidence and human connection. In practice, RIO really is an "appetite framework". People start to want to change their behavior. The more difficult the trade, the harder it is to change behavior. As a trainer, I look for implementable methods. RIO is compact, simple, recognizable and intense. It has certainly refreshed things in our company and has given our people a boost. What I also find a great added value is that it doesn't stay theoretical. Everyone knows those training sessions that make you wonder: Are we actually going to do something with this? With RIO, you feel that people are really involved and go to work with it.'

Commercial duties

Not only customers, but also salespeople differ. Enabling professional sales-people to perform is the shared responsibility of sales and HR management. Furthermore, the *customer experience* is now an important focus for the entire organization and not just the sales and service departments. Commercial tasks, therefore, differ for each prospect, on sales, *customer success*, complaint processing and account management. Initally, an important challenge is to get the right person in the right place.

Insight into the RIO distribution within a team provides immediate tools for dividing sales tasks and letting employees contribute to commercial success, each using their natural strengths.

Koen Vandendriessche: 'A year and a half ago, after testing, we had 24 people who wanted to do front office sales. We now have 45 people, which is almost 50% of all front office staff. Here is a nice anecdote: we recently started with video calls for customers and prospects. So not for service, but for commercial questions. We had opened the assignment and asked who wanted to collaborate on a proof of concept. And I thought: I'll be satisfied with three or four. Instead, I had to hold them back. And that's a good thing. I had room for eight people to do a proof of concept. I had to go up to 14, otherwise I would've disappointed too many people. So, the negative connotation around sales from three years ago is gone. Just gone. That's the biggest change our organization has seen. The front office only wanted to do service and now we're seeing that the "farmer profiles" who once suffered from cold feet are saying: "Go on, give me two more slots for appointments" or "Send that prospect over to me." We've hardly had to replace any people during this transformation process because the "RIO sales story" really hit home.'

Practicing your sales techniques

TRAINING

In addition to filling positions, competence development should be an important focus in any sales team. Skilled sales professionals ensure a high conversion rate of leads to signed contracts. What is the link between the RIO dynamics and sales training? In skills training, RIO forms the bridge between generic sales techniques and the individual motivation needed to successfully apply the tip. Here, we refer to *The Sales Book, For Every Type of Salesperson:*

'Trying to improve your sales results
with a technique that doesn't suit you
is frustrating and doomed to fail.
On the other hand, applying sales techniques
that fit your personal sales style is fun,
comfortable and effective.'

EXAMPLE – COLD CALLING IS A BREEZE

An example from the 'Cold calling, cold trick' course will help make things concrete: When overturning objections during prospecting calls, a rapid response time is crucial. In order to achieve this, we offer participants a choice of three RIO alternatives..

Objection: We already have a regular supplier!

Relational reversal: I'm glad to hear that you already know the advantages of a steady partner. We have no intention of disrupting that collaboration. It is, however, interesting for you to see instead what we can do to complement your partner. What day works for you in the week of 16 November?

Informative reversal: And when was the last time you critically reviewed this supplier? I'll be more than happy to make a comparison of services and prices with you when we see each other. What day works for you in the week of 16 November?

Outgoing reversal: It is, however, dangerous to put all your eggs in one basket. Let me show you what we can do for you if your regular supplier cannot deliver. Does 18 November work for you?

The freedom to choose the wording that aligns best with the novice salesperson lends him the ease and strength to convince the prospect. Advanced colleagues can go a step further and choose the alternative that best suits the customer's style.

For more examples, go to: www.blinc.be/nl/mensen-raken-klanten-maken

Tailored sales coaching

Most sales methods are based on a uniform sales process and generally applicable guidelines. RIO, on the other hand, provides specific instructions for each buyer type when making a custom call (see chapter 7). For that reason, the model becomes particularly illuminating when an identical action by the seller has a positive effect in one conversation and a negative effect in another. Where generic methodologies find themselves confronted with a riddle, RIO offers a logical explanation.

EXAMPLE – THE PITFALL OF OPEN-ENDED QUESTIONS

A sales professional from the media sector asks open-ended questions to the manager of a data center with the intention of finding out her prospect's professional ambitions and personal concerns.

- » Where do you want your organization to stand at the end of this year?
- » How many new customers do you need to attract?
- » What initiatives are you planning in order to generate leads?
- » To what extent are you on schedule?
- » What are your concerns about your plan?

Despite the quality of her questions, the customer drops out during the needs analysis. With the comment 'Tell me what you are selling', the customer suddenly takes control of the conversation and forces the saleswoman to finish the interview early. During the debriefing, the saleswoman indignantly remarks that she did exactly what she was taught during an internal training course in consultative selling. The insight that OCs become impatient with consecutive open-ended questions was new to her, and it provided a concrete explanation for the frustrating experiences she had previously had with similar customers.

───

CUSTOMER CASE: AMPLIFON

Amplifon, a global player in the hearing aid industry, is a company where audiologists serve as the first point of contact for their customers. These people have a distinctly people-oriented profile and attach great importance to the quality of their service. This was especially evident in long sales processes in which information and pampering were the benchmarks. Tine De Boodt is a trainer and audiologist at Amplifon. For her, RIO offers a common language with which she can then convey the commercial message in a way that appeals to everyone.

Tine De Boodt: 'One of our company's objectives was to become more efficient. Our schedules were getting busier and busier and yet we remained stuck in our protocol. We had a fixed sales tool and made every customer go through the process in the same way. That took an enormous amount of time and the results never materialized. We knew something was wrong. We were already working in a very personal way but not one that was personalized to the customer. This changed with RIO. The realization that we don't have to ask open-ended questions to every client, that we should be more direct and don't have to go through the entire tool to be successful was really enriching. The fact that some clients are already prepared to decide during an initial meeting was met with disbelief. Until we tested it in practice and indeed saw that OCs experience multiple appointments as a real waste of time and for that reason simply abandon the purchase. They responded positively to a closing question during an initial appointment and test, which resulted in us saving an enormous amount of time for both our customer and our audiologists.'

A common language for internal communication

Each profession has its jargon, each domain a frame of reference. It facilitates internal communication. For the business aspects in sales there are terms that all sales professionals know: *ideal customer profile*, *customer journey*, *funnel* and *closing ratio* are just a few examples. The human aspects in sales, however, lack the same sort of clarity and everyone tries to describe the customer interaction using their own vocabulary. The RIO model ensures that the human component can be captured in a sales conversation. What was previously only tangible as an easy or difficult customer interaction is now objectified and typical fragments from the dialogue can be discussed.

CUSTOMER CASE 1

A client from the financial sector went a step further in creating recognizable jargon and worked with us to produce three avatars that symbolized RIO client types. From simple videos, internal employees were excited about 'differentiated' sales and readily received applicable information about the pros and cons of Relational Rudy, Informative Iris and Outgoing Oscar (created by graphic design agency Expliciet).

CUSTOMER CASE: AMPLIFON

Amplifon also noted that the flow of information communicated throughout the organization via the internal newsletter was limited. Updates on products, quarterly figures and targets were lost when shared digitally. Click rates showed that employees only opened the mails occasionally and only clicked through them sporadically. In-depth analysis of the language used in the newsletter using the RIO plug-in, an algorithm developed in collaboration with the University of Antwerp that provides insight into the RIO 'weight' of word usage, then revealed that 43% of the words used were O-, 35% I- and 22% R-language; while previous assessments had shown that 40% of employees were relational, 35.5% informative and 23.5% outgoing.

The RIO algorithm

Using the RIO algorithm, the mismatch between the language of the newsletter and the DNA of the employees was mapped out.

Newsletter language:	43% O	35% I	22% R
Employee behavioral style:	40% R	35,5% I	23,5% O

What researchers at the University of Antwerp had previously observed – the link between click behavior, language use and personality – was confirmed in practice. Employees were not reading the newsletter because the topics and word usage were not adapted to their channel of trust.

The management team followed the advice to add relational authors to the communications team and the positive effect was visible in the short term.

Tine De Boodt: 'In practice, I've noticed that selling occurs faster and that it's fun. If I recognize a customer as an R, I know: if I do this, I will have that effect. If I pamper them a little more, they will appreciate it and be more at ease. If it's an I, watch out, I'll need more space in my schedule and they'll ask a lot of knowledge questions. I also know that I will enjoy it, because it feeds my own I. And then if it's an O, I enjoy it now too because it's clear as soon as he walks in. He wants a strong coffee, there we go – it's even become funny in contrast to the old days when I used to dread conversations with that type of customer...

So I think it's really cool that you know the direction in which scenarios will run. And I think that's the same for our employees. We try to integrate RIO into every course; it's our connecting thread. The people from marketing and sales are also completely on board. We all speak the same "language" now. That's a difference that wasn't there a year ago. I really like that!'

The pros and cons of a sales methodology

Organizations that rapidly expand their sales team often do so using a sales methodology. Having many new people entails a need for structured training in which a uniformity of process and competences can offer stable footing.

The implementation of a sales methodology then involves benefits as well as risks. Successful implementation means shorter *ramp-ups*, or the time it takes for starters to get their first deals. Furthermore, a clear methodology ensures shorter sales cycles and larger orders, which have a direct impact on the bottom line. Failed implementation, on the other hand, results in sales reps falling out of routine and losing time to uncomfortable work. Moreover, professional sales reps do not like to be told what to do. Rules of conduct that are too strict lead to a loss of motivation and authenticity, which is disastrous for winning deals.

What is important when choosing a methodology and how do you maximize its implementation? The answer is simple: sales reps will stay with the process if it helps them close more deals. More sales means more commission, which is an important driver. That brings us to the following question: when does a methodology help score more deals, and what is the link with RIO?

There are 10 sales methods worldwide, of which *SPIN selling*, *strategic selling* and *challenger sales* are probably the best known. We will briefly describe what they stand for and what makes each of them unique.

SPIN SELLING

In the 1980s, Neil Rackham studied 35,000 sales interviews conducted by sales professionals from more than 90 organizations. He observed that top sales professionals are masters in asking questions that invite customers to think honestly about their situation. The questioning progresses through four phases in which first the situation, then the problem, then the implication and finally the customer's needs are each clarified. What then makes *SPIN selling* unique is the sociability with which the questions build on one another, convincing the customer of the solution.

STRATEGIC SELLING

Bob Miller and Steve Heiman developed strategic selling while working at IBM. They established that success is not a coincidence, but instead the logical consequence of a sequence of tasks that are consistently carried out. Strategic selling also attaches great importance to the systematic mapping out of the DMU (*decision making unit*), the key figures within the organization who have an interest in the deal and influence on the decision. Strategic selling was unique in aiming to make sales predictable and reduce the risk of errors.

CHALLENGER SALES

In 2011, Matthew Dixon and Brent Adamson came up with a sales method that shook up the systems of their day. They argued that, in a time of digitalization and autonomous buyers, salespeople who only ask questions no longer offer added value. Sales professionals must be confident experts who 'challenge' the customer's self-designed solutions with smart interventions. The *challenger sales* approach disrupts the customer's thinking process and coaxes unspoken needs out into the open. In this way, the salesperson and customer arrive at new avenues of thought and the sales professional contributes tangible added value.

RIO AND SALES METHODOLOGIES

The attentive reader has probably noticed the parallels between the methodologies described and RIO. Little imagination is needed to understand that SPIN selling has a relational basis, strategic selling informative, and challenger sales outgoing. Nor will it surprise anyone that the biggest fans of each respective method are the sales reps with a corresponding channel of trust. Of course, relational sellers are interested in SPIN selling because this approach appeals to their natural aptitude for questioning. It makes sense that informative salespeople apply strategic selling because of their own preference for structure and process. Obviously, outgoing salespeople are motivated to challenge clients; they were already doing that before the method.

What practical insights should we take into account?

1 Choose the methodology that most closely matches the organization's DNA.
2 Provide a 'translation' of the chosen method to all RIO channels.

CUSTOMER CASE: PARTENA HEALTH INSURANCE FUND

Partena Health Insurance Fund has experienced unprecedented commercial growth in recent years. One of the drivers behind this expansion has been the development of their custom sales methodology, Hartena, which is essentially a highly relational way of approaching customers. Koen Vandendriessche testifies that the Hartena sales approach has not only led to spectacular results, but also to a positive perception of sales among employees who predominantly have a relational channel of trust.

Koen Vandendriessche: 'Today, our RIO coaches have already done three hundred field coaching sessions. That's three hundred commercial conversations with customers that they follow on-site. In that way we embed the methodology. They work with the RIO coaching document for this. RIO ensures that you immediately speak the same language. During conversations they used to speak past one another and couldn't put their finger on exactly why. Thanks to a common language, this now goes much more smoothly. This implementation requires time and follow-up from a management team that believes in RIO. It's not: "We're going to do a training session. Take a test, here you have your profile, now do it!" Our RIO coaches also receive monthly supervision from a colleague OM from another region. That is how we monitor quality. The KA's approach has a direct effect on our customers and therefore also on our NPS. A year and a half ago we had an NPS of 13 (!). Today, for physical commercial appointments, we are at an NPS of 72. Those are Apple figures!'

CUSTOMER CASE 2

A market leader in the financial sector has been working with a consultative sales model for years. Despite the customer focus in which the employees are trained, they notice that not every customer has the need for a warm introduction and extensive needs analysis. The major bank realizes that the consultative sales structure they have been using for years has a relational slant. As a result, outgoing and informative customers are not being served to measure. Because it is their strategic ambition to become the most personal bank in Belgium, they have opted to adapt their historically established sales process to include R, I and O methods. RIO is being rolled out for all commercial employees.

CUSTOMER CASE 3

A telecom operator opts for challenger sales, but after three years notices that adoption among sales reps is still substandard. In order to get the sales team to work with the challenger sales method, management must face the choice of either repeating, deleting or 'translating' the method using RIO. Field observations show that the method is, above all, a stretch for relational salespeople. Two of the six principles – 'take control of the conversation' and 'put the customer under pressure' – fundamentally contradict their natural style of behavior. The R-translation of these two principles then becomes:

1 Guide your client through the conversation more smoothly by sharing your goals and intentions at the beginning.
2 Use 'buffer phrases' to make the customer feel that you are challenging him out of good intention. For example: 'I'm sorry if this may sound harsh, but when I think about what is really good for you, I suggest...'

'Shared goals' and 'buffer phrases' are two concrete techniques that offer relational sellers a bridge between challenger sales' uncomfortable principles and their daily practice. Where relational sellers used to reject challenger sales, they now have a modus operandi that enables them to challenge in their own way.

It is clear that RIO is more than just a fun format for getting to know yourself better. Deploying RIO at the right level is not a plaything of which some employees are fans and others not. Working with RIO sets in motion a commercial transformation process in which a company's strategic goals are achieved as a result of the leverage effect on the entire organization.

But enough talking. It is time to dive into the practice and discover RIO with your customer.

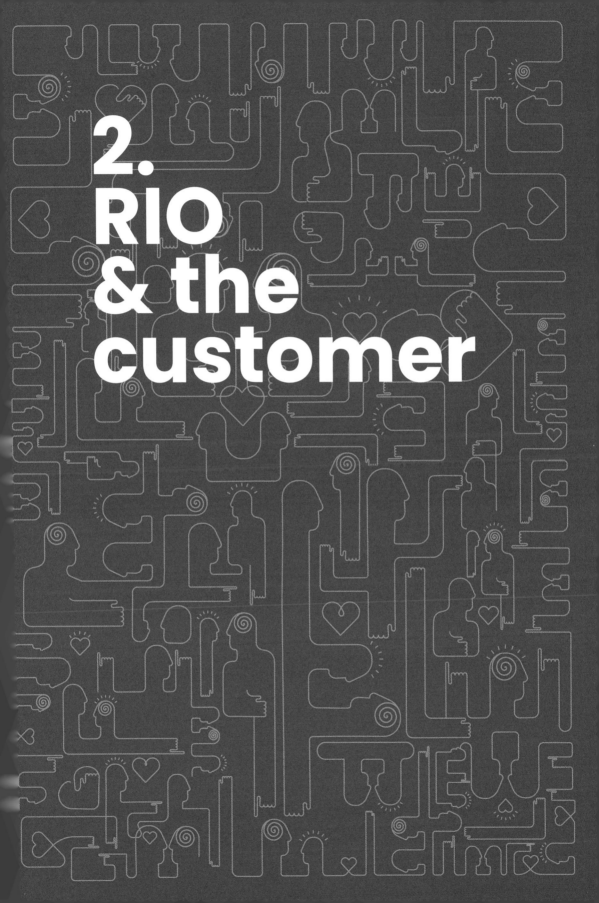

2.
RIO
& the
customer

*How do you recognize
the customer's
channel of trust?*

———

*How do you apply RIO in
marketing throughout
the buyer's journey?*

———

*How do others learn
to sell to every type
of customer through
sales coaching?*

RIO sales skills stand or fall on the ability to scan people. The salesperson needs to develop the attentiveness to pick up relevant clusters and the ability to interpret them. The good news is that RIO is a behavioral model, which means that customer recognition is done on the basis of visible parameters. No sixth sense is required, however, a trained ability to observe is. As with any skill, practice makes perfect and self-confidence grows in practice. Sellers who start working with the tools in this chapter will soon notice that correctly gauging RIO preferences is easier than riding a bike.

'The more recent the trust between conversation partners, the easier it is to scan RIO.'

How do you assess the channel of trust for someone you do not know? A surprising observation is that scanning RIO is actually easiest with someone you have never met before. Which is logical because RIO is a protection mechanism triggered when trust is lacking. Once individuals know and appreciate one another, typical RIO behavior disappears, and people show their full range of behavior. So, the invitation is to dare to trust your first impressions when getting to know someone new!

When is the best time to scan for RIO? There are a number of moments that lend themselves to doing so.

During the sales conversation

The first minutes of a commercial meeting are a gold mine of RIO information. The trip from the reception to the meeting room in B2B or the distance from the front door to the living room table in B2C both contain dozens of clues as to the customer's RIO preference. We have compiled the observations over the years in a document called 'the 10-second scan', which enables salespeople to quickly judge the prospect's RIO type based on targeted observations.

The document is constructed with parameters that are observable or audible. The facial expression, use of voice and body language are the most important. The aim of the 10-second scan is to help render the client's RIO preference measurable. Salespeople should look at their conversation partner and check off their observations, first physically on the document and later, with practice, 'mentally'.

The column that contains most of the prospect's characteristics is the client's RIO preferred channel.

—————

THE 10-SECOND SCAN

R	I	O
• Heartfelt impression • Easy smile • Open look • Displays positive emotions • Looks relaxed • 'I wouldn't hurt a fly' vibe	• Serious impression • Inquiring look • Does not display emotions • Expressionless • 'I'll wait and see' vibe	• Resolute impression • Strong eye contact • Displays positive and negative emotions in their face • Open book • Broad smile • 'Don't toy with me' vibe
• Leans towards the speaker • Often nods approvingly when listening • Calm gait • Rounded and easy arm movements • Flowing hand movements • Lets others enter doorways and elevators before them	• Maintains physical distance • Jumps and pulls back from physical contact • Limited movements • Stiff gait • Few arm and hand movements unless for emphasis	• Direct approach • Short and quick movements • Quick and energetic gait • Impresses with their physical presence • Loud movements: stomps when walking, opening doors • Uses a lot of strength
• Soft voice • Approving sounds • Speaks slower • Need many words to get to a point • Enjoys talking about private matters • Speaks openly about their needs • Likes to listen	• Monotonous voice • Speaks in bullet points: first, second, on the one hand, on the other, etc. • Business facts and information • Asks detail questions • Does not like talking about private matters at all	• Loud voice • Takes the floor • Speaks quickly • Gives short answers • Has strong opinions • Enjoys challenging

When you do not have enough distinct visual clues from customers, it is worth testing the waters with the following question. The reaction speaks volumes.

'How was the drive?'	'How was the drive?'	'How was the drive?'
• Heartfelt account: 'Fine, thanks for asking', followed by an elaborate and animated description	• Awkward answer with a factual description of the situation on the motorway	• Short answer, with the intention of skipping the question: 'Fine'

Before the sales conversation

In addition to the physical 10-second scan, it is possible to obtain an indication of the client's RIO preference before the call. This has the advantage that a sales-person with a corresponding RIO profile can be chosen to approach the client or that the sales professional can prepare with the right profile in mind.

Despite the proactive client assessment methods described below, it is always a good idea to thoroughly prepare for the interview from all RIO angles, so that there are no surprises. A cross-check of the outcome from the various methods gives the best predictive result.

――――

GAUGING RIO BASED ON DATA FROM THE CRM SYSTEM

Customer has previously purchased products or services for comfort, peace of mind, well-being or out of sympathy	Customer has previously purchased products or services for reasons of risk reduction, certainty of return, price-quality ratio	Customer has previously purchased products or services for profit, savings, added efficiency and results
The system contains reports of tardiness in administrative obligations	The system contains reports of content-related detail questions	The system contains reports of complaints about the speed of delivery and execution

GAUGING RIO BASED ON E-MAIL CORRESPONDENCE

• Use of greetings at the beginning and end of each e-mail, even when the message is short	• Formal greeting and signature: Dear Mr., sincere regards, sincerely	• Short e-mails without introduction or signature
• Use of first name in signature	• Long e-mails with many details and numbers	• Action-oriented wording
• Many white lines in e-mail	• E-mail with instructions, links and comparisons	• Use of power words and exclamation points
• Cautious language use: I think, in my opinion, would it, maybe, possibly	• Logically built e-mail with paragraphs and structure	• E-mails consisting of one or two words, such as: Okay! Deal! On it!
• Informal or personal signature: cheers, have a lovely weekend	• Preference for communication via e-mail	• E-mails consisting of one run-on paragraph
	• Sign off with first and last name	• E-mails consisting solely of a subject line
		• Type in red, with exclamation marks and/or in all caps

GAUGING RIO BASED ON LINKEDIN

LinkedIn is the modern professional's passport. Not only does it provide information about a person's professional path, it is also a source of RIO clues. Here, we will deal with the text and photo separately.

TEXT

Together with Textgain[4], a spin-off from the University of Antwerp specialized in *natural language processing*, and traicie[5], an artificially intelligent solution for automated personality detection, we researched the link between personality and language use for three years. The hypothesis was that character dimensions are present in the way people write, the words they use and the way they construct sentences. Several scientific research papers[6] had already shown that certain personality traits can be predicted automatically based on text fragments. The analysis of hundreds of biographies, e-mails and interviews revealed a number of striking findings. We can distinguish the three RIO types from one another in terms of word use, sentence structure and text length. This means that prior to a sales conversation it is possible to be well prepared, not only in terms of content, but also in terms of form. Which type of person will I be dealing with in the future and how can I adjust my sales process accordingly? We built an algorithm and a corresponding web browser extension to predict RIO preferences based on online text. Here is a limited selection of the most commonly used words by the different RIO types.

RELATIONAL WORDS

Supporting, Sustainable, Personal, Collaboration, Advising, Partnerships, Added value, People who have a… (Problem/Interest), Helping, Relationship, Service, Making the difference, Benefit, Need, Satisfaction, Passion for, Empathy, Unique, Change, Internal, Authentic, Unconscious/underlying, Connection, Special, Intuitive, Efficiency, Atypical, Not another …, Individuality, Distinction, In-depth, Human, Easy, Effortless, Naturally, Sympathetic, Flow, Open, Guiding, Winning over, Freedom, Space to, Spontaneous, Atmosphere, Respectful, Fluent

STATEMENTS BY WELL-KNOWN RELATIONAL PEOPLE

The feeling behind these relational words can also be found in quotes from some well-known relational entrepreneurs.

'Daring to show vulnerability is also
a source of strength, creativity, decisiveness
and energy that can lead to success.'

– JOOST CALLENS, DURABRIK

'I always visit potential clients myself.
That way I can get to know the case personally.
I also know every optician I work with by name.
The collaboration is very close, that's the way I prefer it.'

– ELINE DE MUNCK, DEUX

'Consciousness without love is poor but love
without consciousness is dangerous.
For me, these are two important core values
by which I try to live: love for my profession,
for people, for my family, for the world, but also
from consciousness. I try to connect those two.'

– WOUTER TORFS, SHOES TORFS

INFORMATIVE WORDS

Responsible for, Improving, Structure, Quality,
Professional, Legal obligations, Compliance,
Integrity, High priority, Principle, Critical,
Assessing, Skilled, Values and norms, Excellent,
Strategy, Returns, Process, Planning, Expertise/
knowledge, Analysis, Technology, Interested in,
Market, Market research, Domain, Role, Special-
ist, Scientific, Tendency, Tools, Trust, Long term,
Account management, Certain, Experience,
Coordination, Proven, Committed, Concrete,
Task-oriented, Clear, Commitment, Engage-
ment, Dedication

STATEMENTS BY WELL-KNOWN INFORMATIVE PEOPLE

'We're not blind to the risks.
If we miss a trend, we should be looking
at ourselves and not a supplier.'

– BART CLAES, JBC

'Only my friends thought
my physics jokes were funny.'

– LIEVEN SCHEIRE, MEDIA FIGURE

'Optimists are ill-informed pessimists.'

– BART DE WEVER, POLITICIAN

OUTGOING WORDS

Efficiency, Reporting achievements and results, Productivity, Brands, Results-driven, Strengths, Activities, Networking, Winner, Doer, Achievements, Solution-focused, Resilient, Dynamic, Positive, Effective, Practical, Strong, Leader, Energetic, Persuasive, Fast, Execution, Hands-on/No-nonsense, Powerful, Persevering, Smashing, To a fault, Initiative, Daring, Challenge, Innovative, Fun, Super, New, Always, Extremely, State-of-the-art, World leader in the field of, Future-oriented, Innovator, Never boring, Creative, Infinite possibilities, Fantastic, Super

QUOTES FROM WELL-KNOWN OUTGOING PEOPLE

'An entrepreneur is someone who jumps off a cliff without a parachute and builds a plane for himself on the way down.'

– REID HOFFMAN

'How do you know when applying for a job if someone is passionate and fits into the team? Call it a feeling! We want the applicant not only to come and work for us because of our mission, but also to have a clear idea of where he or she wants to have an impact in the job within our company.'

– YNZO OF SANDS

'If you read about everything I do, you'd think

I was abnormal. But I'm not abnormal. I'm just incredibly

passionate and very curious. Had you told me

20 years ago that I was going to start a company

in payment technology solutions (Clear2Pay, red.),

I would have had a good laugh. I see a problem,

and I want to solve it. Over and over and over again.'

– YOURS YELS

PHOTO

Our years of experience in working with salespeople and analyzing their online presence has shown that a professional's LinkedIn picture is an important predictive indicator of their RIO preference. We will describe the most significant indicators for each channel of trust.

RELATIONAL INDICATORS

Puppy eyes
Professionals with a gentle look often belong to the relational group. Relational people like to have pleasant contact with everyone and not to intimidate others. They, therefore, prefer a photo without piercing eye contact.

Indirect photo
Looking down or away from the camera is an indicator of a relational channel of trust. Relational people do not want to be ordinary and express their unique personality in a non-shocking way. An atypical photo is part of that.

Modest smile

Relational people appreciate that you do not toot your horn too loudly and profile yourself sincerely. They choose a natural photo with a modest smile, and not the *Colgate* version.

INFORMATIVE INDICATORS

Serious look

Informative people find it important to radiate professionalism and a sense of responsibility. They avoid playful or pronounced smiles in their photos for a professional context.

Strike a pose!

Prospects who strike a professional pose while taking their profile picture often have the informative channel of trust. These prospects find it important to underline their expertise and consciously consider how best to convey this image.

Black and white bespoke suit

In line with their logical and straight-thinking style, informative people prefer to be professionally photographed in business clothing with black and white contrast.

And... action!

Outgoing professionals are proud of their dynamism and action-oriented attitude. And what better way to capture that than with a picture in full action?

Rise and shine!

Professionals who look straight into the camera and smile with their teeth often demonstrate the outgoing channel of trust. These people appreciate a healthy dose of self-confidence and find it important to radiate that online.

Head tilted

We do not have a conclusive explanation for this, but extensive observation shows that outgoing people, more so than any other, often opt for a photo with their head tilted. The explanation probably lies in the aversion that outgoing people feel towards conservatism and stagnation.

The proactive reader will have already drawn the link: all the listed indicators are of course applicable when bringing your own RIO profile into focus. This will be discussed in detail in chapter 8.

6 THE RIO BUYER'S JOURNEY

61

PART 2 RIO & THE CUSTOMER

Hopefully, the previous chapter brought the RIO customer types to life. It is time to make things practical in marketing and sales!

It is clear that customers today are looking for a unique buying experience. Sellers are well advised not only to live up to the buyer's expectations, but to far exceed them. In this chapter we will describe in detail what the unique desired experience (UDE) of each RIO customer is, which dos and don'ts should be taken into account and how the customer can be guided to a positive purchase decision.

Before we work out the different RIO customer types in detail, it is good to return to basics. What is the definition of a *sustainable commercial transaction* and what is the generic process to achieve it?

We define a sustainable commercial transaction as: the situation in which a person makes an informed decision to purchase a product or service, believing it to be of long-term benefit. The relationship with the seller or sales organization is so positive that the customer shares this with his environment, in person or digitally.

Based on this definition, certain situations do not fulfill the 'sustainable sales' label and we, as RIO creators, distance ourselves from the use of this method for any of the following unethical practices:
» selling under duress;
» selling under pretense;
» selling at prices inconsistent with the market;
» all types of scams.

Marketing and sales

'If you don't like sales, get out of marketing.
If you don't like marketing, get out of sales!'

– JENIFER KERN, CMO QU POS

A statement that applies today more than ever. Digitalization ensures that marketing and sales are linked like the carriages of a high-speed train. The place where the customer encounters marketing is often identical to the place of purchase, the World Wide Web! Customers no longer have to move around, and 'contact' with a salesperson is now done omnidirectionally: by phone, chat, video chat or WhatsApp. In some sectors, customers move autonomously through the purchase process up to and including payment, in others, until just before closing. In all sectors, customers start their purchase journey or *buyer's journey* long before a sales professional comes into play. In their white paper *Bridging the Buyer's Seller Gap*, CSO Insights shares these amazing observations:

70.2% of all customers wait to meet a salesperson until they have insight into their specific needs. 44.2% of all customers go a step further and look for solutions themselves, and 20.2% essentially buy autonomously and only start a conversation to discuss the final details. The customer goes his way and the salesman has to follow! Or not?

Creating added value during the customer journey

The art of sales in 2020 consists of knowing and anticipating the customer process. Top marketers and sales professionals know where the customer is, what he needs and the kind of support that will take him to the next phase. Like an accomplished scout, the sales rep guides his customer through the swamp of choice stress with its associated plethora of options. The customer feels proactively supported, has a 'wow' experience and places his trust and his order with the sales rep. Everyone wins!

But exactly what does the purchasing process, in all its steps, consist of, if we map it out from A to Z? What follows is first and foremost a generic *customer journey* that applies to the statistically 'average' customer. We will then go through the differentiated journeys from the perspective of the RIO customer profiles. In each, the focus is on what the marketer and the sales rep can do to actively guide the customer through the process, while at the same time providing him with a unique buying experience.

The Buyer's Journey

THE MARKETER/
SALES REP

THE CUSTOMER

MARKETING

Attention
Because the marketer
is spreading a provocative
message...

Attention
... the customer's
attention is drawn.

Consumption
Since the marketer makes
'snackable' content...

Consumption
... the customer
'consumes' that content.

Awareness
Because the content is about
recognizable problems
and ambitions...

Awareness
... the customer becomes
aware of a specific need
or ambition.

SALES

Receptivity
Because the marketer
presents an *attractive
solution*...

Receptivity
... the customer takes
an interest in the product
or service.

Readiness to buy
Because the seller adapts
himself to the customer's
buying style in one-to-one
conversations...

Readiness to buy
... the customer is
prepared to buy.

CUSTOMER SUCCESS

Implementation
Because the seller knows
and discusses the most
common challenges...

Implementation
... the customer starts
using the product or
service with ease.

The RIO buyer's journey

'The secret to successful sales is a personalized application of uniformly valid success principles.'

In recent years, marketers and salespeople have focused on the uniformly valid process described above. In this book we go a step further by customizing this generic process specifically for each RIO customer type. The goal is to give marketers, salespeople and entrepreneurs detailed insight into exactly what RIO customers need for a personalized experience throughout their buyer's journey.

Attention: what triggers the RIO customer type's attention?	What draws attention?	What draws attention?	What draws attention?
	• Emotion • Well-being • Family • Being touched • Comfort • Authenticity • Spirituality • Underdogs • A personal story • Inner transformation • A personal recommendation • Subtle humor • Personal attention • A face-to-face conversation • A personalized e-mail • A friendly 'cold call'	• Relevance • Trends • Studies • Risk • Security • Processes • Graphs • Percentages • Newsfeeds • Internet forums • Lifehacks • Reviews • Overviews • Debates • Wordplay • Informative 'cold mail'	• Brands • Performance • Prestige • Success stories • Timesaving • Last-minute offers • Discounts • Demonstrations • External transformations • Quotes • Strong statements • Injustice • Strength • Surprises • Novelties • Bold 'cold call'

Who do they find interesting?	Who do they find interesting?	Who do they find interesting?
• Friends • 'Ordinary' people • Relief workers • Peace activists • Religious leaders	• Experts • Experienced experts • Scientists • Philosophers • Society critics • Doctors	• Famous faces • Successful people • Top athletes • 'Motivational speakers' • Action heroes
Words in the title that generate interest	Words in the title that generate interest	Words in the title that generate interest
• Feeling... • Connecting... • Comfortable... • Effortlessly... • No worries... • Spontaneous... • Of course... • In your way... • Human... • Luckily, with... • The art of... • Talent... • On a human scale... • In flow... • Noble... • Positive... • Love for... • Inwardly... • Really...	• Five steps to... • Key to... • Why... • Secret of... • Smarter... • How... • Legally... • Reduce the risk of... • Professionally... • History of... • Overview of... • Fallacies... • Systematically... • Predictable... • Evidence-based... • Learning... • Strategically... • Perfectly... • Guidelines for...	• Title starts with verb (reach, win over, stop, start, etc.) • Hyperbolic language (super, great, spectacular, etc.) • More efficient... • Lever for... • More effective... • Boost your... • Never again... • How winners... • The solution to... • Strengthen your... • Always... • Cheaper... • No-nonsense... • Competitive... • Top... • Agile... • Disruptively...

	Visual stimuli • Nature images • Family scenes • Smiling people • Relaxed people • Soft colors	**Visual stimuli** • People in bespoke suits and uniform • Symmetric images • Orderly and tidy environments • People posing • Black and white color scheme	**Visual stimuli** • Moving images • People in action • Victory hand signals • People with pearly white teeth • Bright colors
	Auditory stimuli • Singer-songwriter • Melancholic music • Zen music	**Auditory stimuli** • Classical Music • Electronic music • Complex music jazz/metal • Silence	**Auditory stimuli** • Exciting music • Sensual music • Grunge
Consumption: what kind of content does each RIO type consume?	**Format** • Books • Content from one specific author • White papers • Interviews • Ted Talks • Human interest documentaries • Talk shows • Open-hearted posts • Readers' letters • Autobiographies • Self-tests • Quizzes • How-not-to articles • Results from personal survey • Stories about failure	**Format** • Blogs • News sites • Books • Trade journals • Educational articles • Trade union publications • Research reports • Case studies • Wikipedia contributions • Tutorials • Live webinars • Debates • Historical documentaries • Technical reviews • Comparative studies	**Format** • Vlogs • Podcasts • Audiobooks • Short movies • Renowned magazines • Summaries • Instagram • Twitter • Short tutorials • Recorded webinars • Entrepreneur magazines • Public reports • User reviews • Quick scans • Q&As

| Awareness: what is an insight that drives RIO customer types to act? | • Something can be easier
• Something offers more comfort
• Something has a positive effect on humans
• Something provides more connection
• Something creates more happiness
• Something can be more fulfilling
• Something can be more sustainable
• Something can be more equal
• Something can be more respectful
• Something offers more peace of mind
• Something invites me to grow
• Something creates a better atmosphere
• Something is a cure for emotional pain
• Something can be more loving
• Something can be more authentic
• I can be more myself
• I can be more assertive | • Something can be safer
• Something is more certain
• Something offers more guarantees
• There is a better price/quality
• Something could be smarter
• Something can be cheaper
• Something I thought was wrong
• Something can be more scientific
• Something can be more energy efficient
• Something can be automated
• There is a solution I can better follow up myself
• Something gives me more insight
• I can learn something
• Something can be more qualitative
• Something is unclear
• Something goes wrong | • Something can be more efficient
• Something can be more profitable
• There is a more effective solution
• Results can be better
• Something can go faster
• Top performers do it this way
• I can save
• Greater impact is possible
• There is a one-stop shop solution
• Something makes me better known
• Something makes me the best
• Something puts me in a better light
• Something has to be fairer
• Something can be more powerful
• Something is spectacular
• Something is innovative |
| Receptivity: what type of solutions are RIO customers open to? | • Comfortable solutions
• Sustainable solutions
• Ethical solutions | • Technological solutions
• Monitorable solutions
• Long-term solutions | • Practical solutions
• Quick fixes
• Innovative solutions |

Readiness to buy: how do RIO customers prefer to go through conversations with a salesperson?	See Chapter 8 for a detailed overview of dos and don'ts during sales meetings with RIO customers.		
Implementation: what do RIO customers expect from after-service?	• Readiness to listen • Friendly communication • Recognition of the inconvenience • Carefree	• Digital service channels • Clear procedures • Warranty plan • No extra costs	• 24/7 accessibility • Quick response • Solution-focused attitude • Compensation
Sharing reflex: what will inspire RIO customer types to share?	• Testimonial that adds value or warns others	• Testimonial that is interesting for others in terms of content	• Testimonial that puts the product and the writer of the testimonial in a positive light

Marketers will have their hands full with these insights. It is time to give the salespeople their task in the personalized sales process: the commercial conversation!

7 SELLING TO EVERY TYPE OF CUSTOMER

We are getting to the heart of this book: face-to-face sales to any type of customer. Unlike other sales methodologies, RIO *personality-based selling* is based on a flexible commercial conversation consisting of fundamental building blocks. After all, a static process implies that each customer purchases in an identical way and goes through the same chronological steps. Experienced salespeople know from practice that this is not true. It is *the* reason why guidelines that are too strict 'chafe' in a sales conversation.

In order to arrive at the essential building blocks of commercial service, we ask ourselves the following question: 'A "sustainable commercial transaction," as defined in chapter 6, can only take place when what occurs?'

Logical answers to this question:
- » the salesperson is attuned to the customer.
- » the salesperson and the customer both engage in the conversation.
- » the salesperson knows what the customer wants.
- » the customer knows what the salesperson has to offer.
- » the salesperson knows what the customer thinks of his offer.
- » the match between offer and need is clear.
- » doubts have been clarified and parties have committed.
- » things have been carried out as promised or better.

These *non-negotiables* are the process building-blocks with which a sustainable commercial dialogue is built and can be regarded as crucial check points in the process. The absence of one or more of these fundamental components leads inexorably to the 'sustainable transaction' being compromised.

Generic building blocks

The generic building blocks are the 'what'; the differentiated processes below are the 'how'. What action should the salesperson take in the sales conversation and how does he concretely apply this activity in conversation with a relational, informative or outgoing customer?

A special feature of the RIO method is that the building blocks are fulfilled differently for the different customer types and that their sequence in the process differs. Before we delve into the differentiated processes, however, we will offer extra insight into the generic competencies in each building block.

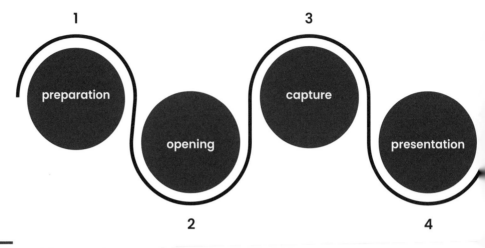

PREPARATION

Good preparation is half the work, especially in today's sales context. Customers expect the sales rep to do the necessary research, familiarize himself with the file and think proactively about problems and solutions. A good preparation includes:

» gathering customer information: online, CRM, media;
» collecting relevant supporting material;
» searching for reference cases;
» assessing the customer's RIO type.

OPENING

Research shows that the 'first impression' in sales is based on the initial seven to ten seconds of the meeting. Failing to create a good first impression means starting the conversation 'behind schedule', with the salesperson's words being critically evaluated for the rest of the meeting. In turn, targeted fine-tuning and establishing a click early on give the salesperson a head start in the process. The salesperson is given credit and the customer covers his doubt and skepticism with the cloak of love.

My first sales manager, an outspoken O-type, put it like this fifteen years ago: 'Clients are like pedal bins. You have to open their lid before you can toss something in. If you don't, all the content falls off.' Despite this statement's lack of elegance, the man did have a point. At the beginning of the conversation, does the customer open his channel of trust or does the salesperson bump up against a closed 'lid'?

The most important part of the meeting phase is creating trust and opening the dialogue. This is done through:

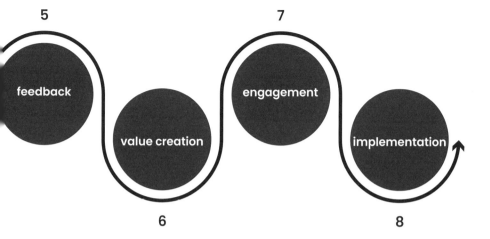

» attuning to the customer type;
» opening the channel of trust;
» positioning the seller and his organization;
» framing of the conversation.

CAPTURE

A customer can never be satisfied with a purchase that fails to fit his needs. It is obvious that at some point in the conversation the salesperson has to glean the customer's interests, needs and ambitions. Uncovering those exact needs is often a continuous process across multiple conversations. In general, top salespeople use the capturing phase in order to understand:
» the customer's functional needs;
» the underlying purchase motives or UDE.
» the decision-making process;
» the decision-making criteria;
» the budget.

PRESENTATION

Unknown is unloved. A customer will not buy anything he does not know exists. In the presentation phase, the sales professional presents his solutions and explains their functionality and assets. Important, here, are the following:
» the explanation of the solution(s);
» the explanation of operation and benefits;
» the use of supporting materials;
» customer enthusiasm.

FEEDBACK

Bearing in mind hyper-personalization, it is utopian to think that the customer will agree with the first solution proposed to him. It is therefore crucial that the seller elicits and captures a response in all its nuances. In this phase:

» ask for feedback;
» elaborate on information;
» refine customer needs.

CREATING VALUE

A large-scale survey of sales and purchasing professionals by Showpad showed that the main reason vendors do not meet their quotas is because their quotas are impossible to meet:

'The inability to articulate unique value.'

Sellers are not successful enough at tailoring their product or service to the customer's situation in such a way that the customer experiences exceptional value. This building block is therefore crucial in the modern commercial process and consists of the following competences:

» demonstrating a detailed understanding of the customer's situation;
» fine-tuning the solution based on feedback;
» articulating its unique value.

ENGAGEMENT

Now we come to the essence of the modern commercial process: positively influencing trust in the collaboration so that both parties commit! Essential activities in this phase are:

» jointly considering potential solutions;
» cognitive and emotional restructuring;
» making conditions concrete;
» expressing commitment.

IMPLEMENTATION

The commercial process in 2020 does not end with the product's delivery, but instead continues until after the customer puts it to use. It is only after the customer has had a positive experience with his purchase and shared it personally or digitally with his environment that the purchase process can be considered complete. In the implementation phase, the following aspects are important:

- » delivery of the purchase;
- » customer guidance during implementation;
- » satisfaction inquiries;
- » invitation to active ambassadorship.

Selling to relational customers

UNIQUE DESIRED EXPERIENCE

'The only way to know if sales profession-als really sell consultatively is to see if they are promoting competitor products in situations where they are better suited.'

– THOMAS WATSON, FORMER CEO OF IBM

Although this statement is a nightmare for many sales managers, it perfectly reflects the relational customer's unique desired experience. Relational customers are looking for a sales conversation that is casual, sincere and advisory. They desire a dialogue in which there is room to really speak openly, lay deep concerns on the table and receive genuine advice from a sales rep who is not thinking about his products or quotas. They crave a conversation in which they are truly heard and sincerely advised, so that they can then follow the adviser's suggestions with peace of mind. Relational customers do not know exactly what they want, but they are willing to follow the person who helps them figure out their needs, feelings and desires.

THE RELATIONAL SALES PROCESS

The relational client's ideal conversation goes as described in the bestsellers on consultative selling. First consult, then suggest a solution!

VISUAL PROCESS

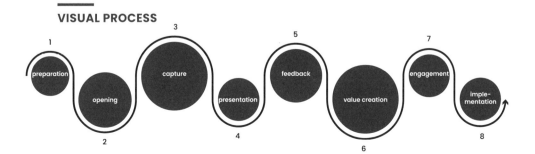

RELATIONAL PREPARATION

'The more you go with the flow, the more you will find that fabulous things start to show up in your life.'

– MANDY HALE, AMERICAN AUTHOR

Generic actions	Relational facts
• Gather customer information beforehand: online, CRM, media • Collect relevant supporting material • Search for reference cases • Assess client's RIO type	• R-customers do not like sales-people who, based on intensive preparation, think they know what the customer's needs are and steer the conversation • R-customers like to feel unique and do not like being compared to a reference case • R-customers are happy to share any information that might be in the CRM system
Fundamental dos	Fundamental don'ts
• Empathize with his or her personal situation • Think about a conversation angle that might be interesting • Plan a warm welcome and empathetic conversation • Know the broad outlines of the current collaboration • Think about what the customer's biggest concerns were in the past	• Write out the entire conversation • Think you know everything • Decide on *the* solution in advance • Lay out presentations and brochures in advance • Fill in order forms or documents to be signed in advance • Schedule a short time slot
Relational statements	Concrete relational tips
• I look forward to our conversation... • Great to be meeting you soon... • I'll have a think about what might be interesting for you... • I'll arrange a comfortable place for us where we can talk undisturbed...	• Book a cozy meeting room • Set aside enough time to have a truly deep conversation • Look up family composition and names in CRM • Put phones on hold and do not answer them during the conversation

'People need to know you care

before they care about what you know.'

– THEODORE ROOSEVELT, FORMER U.S. PRESIDENT

Generic actions	Relational facts
• Tailor yourself to the customer type • Position the seller and his organization • Establish the frame for the conversation	• R-customers like salespeople who, like them, have a quiet, boy/girl-next-door look • R-customers like when the conversation progresses organically • R-customers like to be asked how they see the conversation progressing
Fundamental dos	Fundamental don'ts
• Friendly smile • Sincere small talk • Open posture • Rough sketch of the conversation • Show that you are there to listen to the customer	• Rehearsed behavior (unnatural posture, specific handshake, *Colgate* smile, prepared compliment) • Get directly to the point • Boast with namedropping • Exaggerated enthusiasm
Relational statements	Concrete relational tips
• Welcome. Was it easy to find? • Shall we grab a coffee together? • Tell me, how are you? • How's your family? • What else has happened since we last spoke?	• Set everything aside for a moment so that there is room to connect • Leave presentations and brochures closed for the time being • Plan a conversation on a comfortable sofa rather than at a formal desk

RELATIONAL CAPTURE

'Most people do not listen with the intent to understand;

they listen with the intent to reply.'

– STEVEN COVEY, MANAGEMENT AUTHOR

Generic actions	Relational facts
• The customer's functional needs • The underlying purchase motives or UDE • The decision-making process • The decision criteria • The budget	• R-customers are usually at the very beginning of their buying process and need the vendor to clarify their needs and requirements • R-customers decide during the needs analysis whether they will buy, based on the seller's likeability and listening skills • R-customers are transparent and will share all information openly when kindly asked
Fundamental dos	**Fundamental don'ts**
• Ask open-ended questions regarding the client's perception and priorities • Ask elaborating questions out of genuine interest • Listen, listen and listen • Confirm you have properly understood so that the customer really feels that he has been heard	• Ask questions that are too operational, product or process-oriented • Ask overly critical or direct questions • Directly pick up on the customer's answers and take the floor • Ask questions and leave no room to answer • Declare you have found *the* solution before listening
Relational statements	**Concrete relational tips**
• What's important for you to...? • What do you expect from a partner? • What questions and/or concerns do you have today regarding...? • How do you find the...? • What do you mean? • Allow me to briefly summarize	• Take the time to let your client speak • Really listen to your client! • Do not think what your next answer will be • Always keep an open empathic attitude and follow the customer's flow

'The success of your presentation

will be judged not by the knowledge

you send but by what the listener receives.'

– LILLY WALTERS, PUBLIC SPEAKER

Generic actions	Relational facts
• Explain the solution(s) • Explain how it works and the benefits • Use supporting materials • Get the customer excited	• R-customers are only interested in a personalized presentation in which the salesperson shows that he has listened • R-customers are not interested in strong stories, long references and technical details • R-customers prefer a conversation without a brochure or PowerPoint presentation
Fundamental dos	**Fundamental don'ts**
• Mention only those elements that have a clear link with the client's story • Ensure an ongoing dialogue by frequently testing the customer's feelings about what you say	• Deliver a standard presentation • Include long lists of technical characteristics, references and performance • Over-focus on financial returns
Relational statements	**Concrete relational tips**
• Now that I understand what's important to you, I suggest looking at how our products can help you… • Based on what I've heard, I think it would be interesting for you to… • Let me explain why this is an advantage for you… • What you'll notice is…	• Translate product features into human benefits • Involve the customer in the story, keep the dialogue open • Personalize brochures with a highlighter • Maintain eye contact • Support the story with a live sketched drawing • Pepper your presentation with human anecdotes

RELATIONAL FEEDBACK

'Feedback is a gift.

Ideas are the currency of our next success.

Let people see you value both feedback and ideas.'

— JIM TRINKA, CHIEF TALENT OFFICER

Generic actions	Relational facts
• Ask feedback questions • Elaborate information • Refine customer needs	• R-customers only give feedback if the seller allows enough time and space for it • Sellers should explicitly ask for negative feedback, if they do not, the R-customer will only give positive feedback • R-customers appreciate it when the salesperson takes their emotional feedback seriously • R-customers nod and smile often. That does not mean they agree with everything!
Fundamental dos	Fundamental don'ts
• Explicitly invite the customer to give feedback • Actively ask for 'negative' feedback • Allow plenty of room for customer feedback	• Deny the customer the time and space to express his objections and concerns • Immediately go on the defensive • Minimize objections
Relational statements	Concrete relational tips
• How does that seem to you? • What's your first reaction here? • What are your concerns? • What would you have liked to see?	• Tell the customer that you always like to hear positive *and* negative feedback • Give the customer the feeling that he is helping by sharing feedback • Have an open attitude when receiving the feedback

'Don't find customers for your products,

find products for your customers.'

– SETH GODIN, FORMER DOT COM DIRECTOR

Generic actions	Relational facts
• Demonstrate detailed understanding of the customer situation • Fine-tune the solution based on feedback • Highlight unique value	• For R-customers, the most important value of a product or service lies in extra comfort, peace of mind, connection, self-development, positive atmosphere and well-being • R-customers greatly appreciate it when the sales rep incorporates their feedback and demonstrates that the offer is made to measure
Fundamental dos	Fundamental don'ts
• Return the essence of the feedback received to the customer • Make targeted adjustments to the proposal so that it perfectly matches the customer's wishes • Link the value of your proposal directly to comfort, peace of mind, connection, self-development, positive atmosphere and well-being	• Ignore the feedback given • Repeat the standard offer • Give the customer the feeling that he is being difficult
Relational statements	Concrete relational tips
• What I understand from your feedback is... • Let's see how we can create a solution tailored to your needs...	• Build up the proposal step by step, identify the personalized benefits at each step • Delete a number of elements from the original proposal that are no longer relevant

RELATIONAL ENGAGEMENT

'How you sell matters. What your process is matters.
But how your customers feel when they engage
with you matters more.'

— TIFFANI BOVA, SALESFORCE SPEAKER

Generic actions	Relational facts
• Jointly consider potential solutions • Cognitive and emotional restructuring • Make conditions concrete • Express commitment	• R-customers are reluctant to make things concrete • R-customers appreciate a sales-person who gives them the feeling they can say 'no' at any time • R-customers often think their decision disappoints others • R-customers need positive encouragement
Fundamental dos	**Fundamental don'ts**
• Take emotional considerations se-riously and discuss stress openly • Make the customer dream positively • Resolve practical concerns • Show empathy for buying stress • Make it easy for the customer to sign up	• Rationally refute their concerns • Push your own preferences • Create time pressure with deadline • Give last minute discounts • Push and arouse guilt • Use scarcity: 'These are the last pieces...' • Heavy administrative procedures
Relational statements	**Concrete relational tips**
• Let's have a look at what the options are and which one you prefer... • It's normal for you to find it difficult, but imagine that... • You could also look at it this way... • When would you be able to take this step? • We take care of all practical matters. Shall I arrange it for you? • You're going to see that you'll be satisfied with your purchase...	• Speak in 'we' terms • Lighten the atmosphere with some humor • Avoid sitting directly opposite the customer; side by side or in a corner works better • Use emotion-oriented jargon in-stead of cognitive-oriented jargon: 'Do you feel good about that solution?' instead of 'What do you think of that solution?' • Sincerely encourage the customer

'If you don't appreciate and take care
of your customers, someone else will.'

– JASON LANGELLA, CHIEF MARKETING OFFICER –

TAMPA SEO AGENCY

Generic actions	Relational facts
• Deliver the purchase • Accompany the customer during implementation • Verify satisfaction • Invite the customer to be an active ambassador	• R-customers hate red tape and 'problems' during implementation • R-customers share positive feed-back when they are truly satisfied; they prefer not to be asked
Fundamental dos	**Fundamental don'ts**
• Take practical concerns off the customer's hands • Kindly and attentively listen to the customer in the case of complaints • Do not be difficult in case of return • Be easy to reach for after-service	• Small print • Unpleasant surprises upon delivery • Cumbersome customer service procedures • Blunt response to complaints
Relational statements	**Concrete relational tips**
• We want to see you smile... • I'll take care of that for you... • Don't worry, that's included... • I'm sorry to hear that... • Our apologies for the inconvenience... • Thank you very much for your feedback...	• Be reachable as a contact person • Call to see if everything is okay • Recognize the personal inconvenience and thank the customer explicitly for feedback • Prepare a customer testimonial text on your own and ask if you can share it

Selling to informative customers

UNIQUE DESIRED EXPERIENCE

'Professionalism is not the content of your job, but the way you do it. It requires integrity and consistency to always do the things that benefit tho customer and the business, even on the days when you don't feel like it or nobody's watching.'

– ERIC LIPPERT, SOFTWARE EXPERT AND AUTHOR

How perfectly the business world would run if each salesperson were an expert on content *and* a virtuous professional. In his unique desired experience, the informative customer is not looking for human proximity, but instead for the most reliable solution to his problem and a supplier who can guarantee correct service. The purchase process must be clear, the interaction professional and the implementation as agreed. More than anything, the informative customer wants to learn from a supplier with superior knowledge, experience and know-how and one with a clear path to the solution. Complex, emotionless and risk-free. Clear, right?

THE INFORMATIVE SALES PROCESS

In the ideal informative sales conversation, the general product presentation comes before the capture phase, so as to enable I-customers to assess the

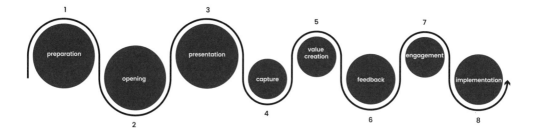

professionalism and quality of the supplier before sharing their problems and
ambitions. An I-participant in our training expressed it as follows: 'Surely
you'd ask a doctor for his diploma before undressing?'

INFORMATIVE PREP

'Give me six hours to chop down a tree

and I will spend the first four sharpening the axe.'

– ANONYMOUS

Generic	Informative facts
• Gather customer information beforehand: online, CRM, media • Collect relevant supporting material • Search for reference cases • Assess customer's RIO type	• I-customers attach particular importance to preparation; they know their situation and the market well and expect the same from sellers • I-customers appreciate it when the vendor proactively gathers relevant documentation, presentation material and reference cases • I-customers are discrete in the information they share online, proactively identifying the customer's RIO type is difficult
Fundamental dos	**Fundamental don'ts**
• Familiarize yourself with the client's file • Gather relevant information and documentation • Look up market trends and evolutions • Map out the competition • Prepare answers to possible questions • Prepare a presentation	• Be unprepared • Lack clear goals and structure for the meeting • Have no relevant leads
Informative statements	**Informative tips**
• A standard introductory meeting with us takes 40 minutes • Can I project a number of slides in your meeting room? • May I ask you to bring this information with you?	• Send a meeting invitation with agenda items to the client • Inform the client how to prepare for the meeting • Share your organization's website with the customer in advance

INFORMATIVE OPENING

'Professionalism means consistency of quality.'

— FRANK TYGER, PUBLISHER AND CARTOONIST

Generic	Informative facts
• Tailor yourself to the customer type • Position the seller and his organization • Provide a frame for the conversation	• I-customers are most impressed by salespeople who radiate professional mastery • A clear framework at the beginning of the conversation is extremely important for I-customers • A formal acquaintance and the salesperson's background are a must
Fundamental dos	**Fundamental don'ts**
• Wear business attire • Begin with a formal introduction and exchange business cards • Clearly set out the agenda with timing • Provide your professional background • Present an organigram of your company	• Arrive late • Take an overly familiar approach • Engage in banal small talk (the weather, the weekend, traffic jams, etc.) • Wear casual or sloppy clothing • Start with a spontaneous conversation opener
Informative statements	**Informative tips**
• I'll give you my business card • Allow me to go over how I've prepared the structure for our meeting • Is it still correct that these are the items on the agenda? • I've set aside an hour for this conversation, does that work for you? • Our organization has been going for 10 years now, I myself have a background in…	• Maintain 1-meter physical distance • Address the customer as Mr/Ms. • Inform yourself concerning the local etiquette for international meetings • Go over the agenda and provide room for input from the customer

INFORMATIVE PRESENTATION

'Where there is shouting, there is no true knowledge.'

– LEONARDO DA VINCI

Generic	Informative facts
• Set out the solution(s) • Explain operation and benefits • Use supporting materials • Get the customer excited	• I-customers prefer to start with a clear presentation by the salesperson • I-customers are well advanced in their buying process when they meet a salesperson; they have insight into their needs and possible solutions; they use the presented information as a quality test of the selling organization • I-customers value professional maturity over enthusiasm
Fundamental dos	**Fundamental don'ts**
• Give a structured presentation of organization • Provide an overview of the product range • Explain how the products or services operate • Offer objective information about the strengths and weaknesses of the products	• Engage in super positive storytelling • Jump around from one subject to the next • Explain obvious issues in detail • Ask too many questions at this stage
Informative statements	**Informative tips**
• Here you can see a timeline extending from the creation of our organization... • The vision we have is... • The trends we see in the market... • Our R&D department collaborates with the University of... • The way we position ourselves in the market...	• Prepare a presentation • Temper your enthusiasm and humor • Use charts in your presentation • Mention that you would like to give the presentation • Use professional presentation tools

INFORMATIVE CAPTURE

'Objectivity is understanding a situation undistorted by emotion or personal bias.'

– ROBERT FERGUSON, MANAGEMENT CONSULTANT

Generic	Informative facts
• Understand the customer's functional needs • Understand the underlying purchase motives or UDE • Understand the decision-making process • Understand the decision criteria • Find out their budget	• I-customers respond best to business questions that gauge their functional needs • I-customers do not want to immediately lay all of their cards on the table regarding their budget and do not appreciate it when asked about it directly
Fundamental dos	**Fundamental don'ts**
• Ask targeted questions demonstrating expertise and preparation • Structure your questions with a clear purpose and framework • Introduce questions with observation, market evolution or trend • Ask questions that make the customers think • Ask questions about their decision-making process	• Ask questions about things you could have found online • Ask banal questions • Ask many questions • Ask personal questions • Answer for your customer • Make assumptions
Informative statements	**Informative tips**
• I saw on your website that you…? • In preparation for this conversation, I read… How do you see this? • The market shows that…; what are your expectations? • The reason I'm asking this is… • What we see in the marketplace is… Did you also notice that? • What have you found regarding…? • How are decisions made in your organization around…?	• Follow the agenda item by item • Explain why you are asking something so that the customer understands the reasoning behind the question • Indicate how many slides you are going to show and number them so that the customer can maintain oversight • Mention that the customer will receive your presentation

'All which is beautiful and noble

is the result of reason and calculation.'

– CHARLES BAUDELAIRE, POET AND ART CRITIC

Generic	Informative facts
• Demonstrate a detailed understanding of the customer situation • Fine-tune the solution with the customer in mind • Highlight unique value	• I-customers are looking for objective Information and appreciato it when the seller explicitly states what a product cannot do • I-customers recognize where things can go wrong and are impressed by a salesperson who anticipates from experience and know-how • I-clients are not early adopters; they choose solutions whose effectiveness can be substantiated with figures
Fundamental dos	Fundamental don'ts
• Compare similar products • Make quantitative price-quality statements • Use graphs and statistics • Provide detailed information	• Make instinctive statements • Compare different contexts • Employ pseudoscience
Informative statements	Informative tips
• What we do with customers similar to you is... • Analysis shows that this is the best approach for you; let me explain why... • The parameters that we take into account in your case are... • A business case will show that...	• Link your product to the themes: risk management, return, working smarter, automation, objectivity and security • Create an ROI calculator for your business that you can use live with the customer • Show that you are fully aware of the legal framework • Indicate the sources of your information

INFORMATIVE FEEDBACK

'Examine the content of what is said, not who speaks.'

– AFRICAN PROVERB

Generic	Informative facts
• Ask for feedback • Elaborate on information • Refine customer needs	• I-customers are not open books; their point of view can best be deduced from the additional questions they ask • I-customers prefer to weigh up on their own but appreciate it when a salesperson with knowledge can contribute • I-customers need time to process information and therefore do not provide immediate feedback
Fundamental dos	Fundamental don'ts
• Ask if something is still unclear • Ask whether the information provided was in line with expectations • Respect the customer's vision and knowledge	• Repeat the sales pitch or keep talking • Deprive the customer of time to organize his thoughts • Assume silence is consent • Link any doubts to the customer's lack of understanding: 'You misunderstand me...'
Informative statements	Informative tips
• Is everything clear? • What else would you like to know? • That's an interesting thought, what gives you that idea? • Good that you mention that. It's just that...	• Think about your answers and show the evidence • Take time to clarify all objections point by point • Only answer critical questions with full knowledge of the facts • Involve internal experts when you do not immediately know the answer

'Nothing consoles and comforts like certainty does.'

– AMIT KALANTRI, WEALTH OF WORDS

Generic	Informative facts
<ul><li>Jointly consider potential solutions</li><li>Cognitive and emotional restructuring</li><li>Make conditions concrete</li><li>Express commitment</li></ul>	<ul><li>I-customers are smart negotiators; they know the fine details of their file</li><li>I-customers do not decide in the moment but instead plan their decision-making process</li><li>I-customers attach great importance to contracts and want to know the impact of each sentence</li></ul>
Fundamental dos	Fundamental don'ts
<ul><li>Neatly list the pros and cons</li><li>Make a concrete calculation of the relevant data</li><li>Draw up a detailed quote with the terms and conditions of collaboration</li><li>Offer a substantiated staggered discount</li><li>Forward information and agree on a concrete follow-up date</li></ul>	<ul><li>Make irrelevant references</li><li>Employ transparent closing tricks</li><li>Quote with too little information</li><li>Argue on emotion</li><li>Make an immediate closure without a reflection period</li><li>Stalk without content</li><li>Fail to comply exactly with the follow-up agreements that were made</li><li>Remain vague about the next steps</li></ul>
Informative statements	Informative tips
<ul><li>Do you have any idea about when you might want to make a decision on this?</li><li>Are you convinced of the quality?</li><li>The guarantees we offer are...</li><li>What we do by default at this point...</li><li>Does a pilot project make sense to you?</li><li>Let's schedule our next appointment to...</li></ul>	<ul><li>Provide the contact details of a reference customer in a similar context</li><li>Go through the contract and make adjustments (contracts are very sensitive)</li><li>Home in on warranties</li><li>Make a reverse planning</li><li>Forward the bundled information</li></ul>

INFORMATIVE IMPLEMENTATION

'Excellent customer service is the number one job in any company. It is the personality of the company and the reason customers come back. Without customers, there is no company.'

– CONNIE ELDER, CEO PEAK 10 SKIN

Generic	Informative facts
• Deliver the purchase • Accompany the customer during implementation • Verify satisfaction • Invite the customer to be an active ambassador	• I-customers attach great importance to agreements and deadlines, also from a legal point of view • I-customers live up to their commitments in order to ensure proper implementation
Fundamental dos	**Fundamental don'ts**
• Make an administrative file • Sign all the required documents and their necessary copies • Respect any agreements made	• Disregard the deadline • Use complex communication lines • Respond emotionally to complaints • Fail to comply with legal obligations
Informative statements	**Informative tips**
• I'll send you a copy of your client file • You can follow the status of your purchase online • The way we're going to fix this for you is..:	• Assemble a project team for complex implementations • Make a clear calendar of what the coming months will look like and what the customer can expect • Feed the customer with interesting articles and facts • Do not stalk the customer with cross-sell and up-sell items

Selling to outgoing customers

UNIQUE DESIRED EXPERIENCE

'If you can't stop thinking about it, buy it!'

— ANONYMOUS

Deal! When can you deliver – today? The outgoing customer's unique desired experience is simple. Speak convincingly, offer a competitive price and deliver quickly! O-customers want an efficient and effective solution to their problem. No time to lose, the only way is forward. Outgoing customers like people who think ahead and act as quickly as they do. Solving a problem before it occurs? Super! Time saved! No blah-blah-blah and lots of boom, boom, boom. *Let's go!*

THE OUTGOING SALES PROCESS

The outgoing customer's ideal conversation contradicts all consultative sales models. O-customers do not want you to question them, they want you to knock their socks off with a fantastic solution! That is why in the outgoing sales process, the presentation stands at the forefront. It is only after a strong pitch that the O-customer will invest time in a conversation that is short and powerful. Convince me why it should interest me, tell me what it costs and get it right. Full stop!

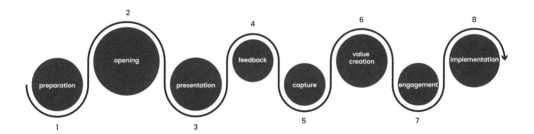

OUTGOING PREPARATION

*'Opportunity does not waste time
with those who are unprepared.'*

– IDOWU KOYENIKAN, BUSINESS AUTHOR

Generic	Outgoing facts
• Gather customer information beforehand: online, CRM, media • Collect relevant supporting material • Search for reference cases • Assess customer's RIO-type	• O-customers are impressed by salespeople who think ahead, know their business needs and have a solution ready to go • O-customers know their important business metrics and appreciate it when the sales rep knows them too • O-customers like to be convinced of the impact of a solution based on impressive references
Fundamental dos	**Fundamental don'ts**
• Know the customer's main challenges • Prepare a solution to the customer's problem • Provide a concise overview • Bring the order form or contract along • Be prepared for a concrete quote	• Gather many documents and statistics • Prepare lengthy presentations • Take a relaxed and no-obligation approach to the conversation • Schedule a meeting for more than an hour
Outgoing statements	**Outgoing tips**
• See you soon! • I'll walk you through our assets when we see each other	• Dress casual chic • Reserve a parking space for your customer • Make sure everything is ready • Wait for the customer in the entrance hall • Create a one-page overview of your offer

'You never get a second chance

to make a first impression.'

– ANDREW GRANT, BRITISH AUTHOR

Generic	Outgoing facts
• Tailor yourself to the customer type • Position the seller and his organization • Provide a frame for the conversation	• O-customers assess a salesperson very quickly based on dynamism and appearance; a lack of charisma is problematic • O-customers like to come straight to the point • O-clients know what they want; in the introduction, they say what they are looking for • O-clients do not care much for formal introductions and the conversation agenda
Fundamental dos	Fundamental don'ts
• Give a solid handshake • Make strong eye contact • Appear dynamic • Make a successful first impression • Use materials from famous brands • Present yourself with self-confidence	• Give a slack handshake • Look away • Speak with a faint voice • Wear shabby clothes • Make an unfit impression
Outgoing statements	Outgoing tips
• Welcome! Welcome! • I suggest we get straight to the point • Today I would like to introduce you to our top product • You're going to see that with this service we'll be leaving our competitors far behind	• Prepare a strong pitch • Take charge of the conversation • Infect the customer with your enthusiasm • Say what the customer can get out of the meeting today

OUTGOING PRESENTATION

'Any fool can know, the point is to understand.'

– ALBERT EINSTEIN

Generic	Outgoing facts
• Set out the solution(s) • Explain operation and benefits • Use supporting materials • Get the customer excited	• O-customers want you to know their context • O-customers want their socks knocked off by the efficiency and effectiveness of the solution offered • O-customers hate it when the seller is not convinced of his own solution
Fundamental dos	**Fundamental don'ts**
• Deliver a brief and concrete pitch • Make the customer face the facts • Know powerful benchmark figures • Go over your offer's practical advantages	• Begin with long introductions • Prepare heavy-duty slide decks • Make obvious statements • Speak in a monotonous style
Outgoing statements	**Outgoing tips**
• We all know that... • The problem with that is... • Figures say that... • Our solution is... • Our customers are... • Your advantage is... • That's how you win... • The investment pays for itself in...	• Show that you know your client's challenges • Make your client think with surprising insights • Show that you have done your homework numerically • Let the customer salivate from your solution • Make your solution concrete and practical

'Feedback is the breakfast of champions.'

– KEN BLANCHARD, MANAGEMENT CONSULTANT

Generic	Outgoing facts
• Ask for feedback • Elaborate on information • Refine customer needs	• O-customers wear their hearts on their sleeves and immediately indicate what does and does not interest them • O-customers are open to being vigorously challenged on the misconceptions they might have
Fundamental dos	**Fundamental don'ts**
• Immediately respond to customer questions and comments • Make bold and substantiated replies • Quickly understand what the customer does and does not want • Rapid interaction with the customer	• Feel personally attacked • Immediately change your opinion • Act in a pleasing manner • Avoid discussion
Outgoing statements	**Outgoing tips**
• I disagree with that... • What you're forgetting is that... • Did you know that this way you'll be much faster at...? • How we solve that is by...	• See the quick interaction with the customer as a game of table tennis • Challenge yourself to make your sales call with fewer words • Convince yourself that you have the best solution • Find out what the customer wants based on their feedback • Be extremely solution-oriented in the case of customer objections

OUTGOING CAPTURE

'When we live our life as if it were an open book,
we are free in body, mind and spirit.'

– MOLLY FRIEDENFELD, *THE BOOK OF SIMPLE HUMAN TRUTHS*

Generic	Outgoing facts
• Understand the customer's functional needs • Understand the underlying purchase motives or UDE • Understand the decision-making process • Understand the decision criteria • Find out the budget	• O-customers know what they want before meeting a salesperson and find an extensive need-analysis a waste of time • O-customers wear their hearts on their sleeves and immediately indicate what does and does not interest them
Fundamental dos	**Fundamental don'ts**
• Read the client's interest • Flexibly respond to questions that come up • Ask suggestive questions • Ask targeted problem-solving questions: 'In the case of…, do you… or…?' • Ask to-the-point questions • Make focused summary	• Ask overly vague, open-ended questions • Ask transparent questions: 'If you think about… What's important to you?' • Ask obvious questions: (in a parking garage) 'What are you looking for…?' • Ask many questions
Outgoing statements	**Outgoing tips**
• Were you already familiar with our product? • I suppose you…? • I may assume that someone like you is interested in…? • What do you do in the case of…? • Do you do…? • Are you interested in…?	• Find out what the customer wants through a process of active questioning • Show the customer why he should be interested

'The secret to success is no secret.

It's called work your ass off and find a way to add

more value to peoples' lives than anyone else does.'

— TONY ROBBINS, MOTIVATIONAL SPEAKER

Generic	Outgoing facts
• Demonstrate a detailed understanding of the customer's situation • Fine-tune the solution to the customer's needs • Highlight unique value	• O-customers are convinced by arguments about efficiency, financial growth, speed, impact, saving time, brand awareness, prestige and innovation • O-customers do not like cross-selling and up-selling; they know what they want and do not like a seller trying to sell them extra products or services
Fundamental dos	Fundamental don'ts
• Repeat and substantiate the main strengths with concrete results • Share impressive achievements • Show that you have thought about objections in advance • Stick to your point of view	• Beat around the bush • Use lots of text and explanation • Provide theoretical sales stories • Be unconvinced of the product • Change your opinion
Outgoing statements	Outgoing tips
• I stand by it: the best solution for you is... • We see that the most efficient way to work is to... • You're going to get the most out of it when you...	• Be convinced of your product and radiate that • Prepare strong references • Translate features into practical benefits

OUTGOING ENGAGEMENT

'The way to get started is to stop talking and to start doing.'

– WALT DISNEY

Generic

- Jointly consider potential solutions
- Cognitive and emotional restructuring
- Make conditions concrete
- Express commitment

Outgoing facts

- O-customers do like to be told the facts by a vendor they respect
- When they are not convinced of a solution it is difficult to show them otherwise
- O-customers will always try to get a discount 'for the sport of it'
- O-customers decide on the spot

Fundamental dos

- Do not beat around the bush regarding price
- Show your enthusiasm and conviction
- Make a concrete proposal quickly
- See your price as obvious
- Start quickly on practical matters

Fundamental don'ts

- Ditch the brochure or PowerPoint presentation
- Tell them to 'Think it over afterwards'
- Provide a detailed quote
- Make them wait long for an offer
- Shy from closing
- Continue to follow up after clear 'no'

Outgoing statements

- We are convinced that we have the best solution
- What do you think?
- Does this appeal to you?
- We can't get started without a signature, can we?
- Shall I draw up the documents?
- What's stopping you from deciding now?

Outgoing tips

- Maintain strong eye contact
- Provide a 'quick decision' discount
- Calculate the return on investment and inform the customer when his investment starts to generate profit
- Fill in the customer's details on the order form beforehand
- Hold out your hand when making your final offer

'Satisfied customer is the best source of advertisement.'

– C.S. ALAG, AUTHOR

Generic	Outgoing facts
• Deliver the purchase • Accompany the customer during implementation • Verify satisfaction • Invite the customer to be an active ambassador	• O-customers prefer things to be converted into action immediately • O-customers demand a quick communication line and action orientation from the supplier in the case of problems; they hate it when things stall • O-customers are expressive and readily share both positive and negative experiences
Fundamental dos	Fundamental don'ts
• Provide immediate service • Be reachable outside of office hours • Be a one-stop-shop for solutions	• Fail to meet agreements • Forget to call back • Complex service procedures • Miss your deadline • Change previous agreements
Outgoing statements	Outgoing tips
• We'll take care of that! • A partner of ours will arrange that • Feel free to call me outside of office hours	• Ensure continuous attendance • Make sure that problems are solved quickly • Offer compensation in the case of major inconveniences • Establish your limits when it comes to excessive demands

Selling to multiple decision-makers

In B2B sales, a buying committee is more often the rule than the exception. The same also applies to private sales, where there is often more than one interlocutor, for example in real estate, insurance, banking, the automotive industry and others. A relevant question then arises: how to apply RIO during a conversation with several people around the table? Here are some of the most important insights.

THE GOLD STANDARD

When presented with a DMU (decision making unit), it is good to start from the position that each of the three RIO dynamics are represented within the decision-making committee. Even within couples, there are often different RIO preferences. In these cases, the preparation should be based on the gold standard that says the sales presentation should contain relational, informative and outgoing elements in a 33%/33%/33% proportion. It is then a good idea to use RIO as a 'process model' at that point in time, where the first part of the conversation is about 'relating', the middle part about 'informing' and the final part about being 'outgoing'.

The layout of the presentation material is key when applying the gold standard. It must explicitly include binding, factual and decisive sections. Additionally, it is crucial that the seller pays equal attention to each of the three phases, without focusing too much on his 'favorite' part.

ENCOURAGEMENT

The experienced RIO salesperson will quickly recognize the dynamics at play among the various interlocutors. Often the channels of trust are easier to detect because the differences in behavior between people are clear. At that moment, the trained sales rep will know what the 'difficult' elements will be for each of the individual listeners, which parts of the conversation will be less stimulating. It is then good to subtly encourage the person in question by framing the passage. For example, by saying to the O-person in the company: 'We'll zoom in on the dry technical elements in order to be able to better identify the practical benefits later on.' Framing prevents a conversation partner from dropping out during the 'uninteresting' section and confusing the conversation later.

PROFESSIONAL ROLE DOES NOT EQUAL RIO

Decision-making committees are usually composed of people with different professional roles. For example, a DMU can be made up of the directors of operations, HR and finance. Although it is tempting to assume that operations will be outgoing, HR relational and finance informative, we recommend always doing the individual 10-second scan. A customer's professional role does not equal his RIO. Of course, people in similar professional roles have similar functional needs, but these do not determine their personality type. Not all HR managers are relational, not all CEOs outgoing. It is good to separate the professional role and functional needs from the personal channel of trust. Both sources of information should be seen as supplementary when creating an 'ideal customer profile' or marketing persona.

TAKE A COLLEAGUE WITH YOU!

A final tip is very practical and effective: approach the decision-making committee as a pair by taking along a complementary RIO colleague. Ten years of experience in B2B sales shows that this has an immediate leverage effect on the outcome of the conversation!

Although you are stronger with two, it is nevertheless definitely worth getting the best out of yourself. Exactly how to develop yourself, as an individual, into a comprehensive RIO salesperson is something you will learn in the following chapters.

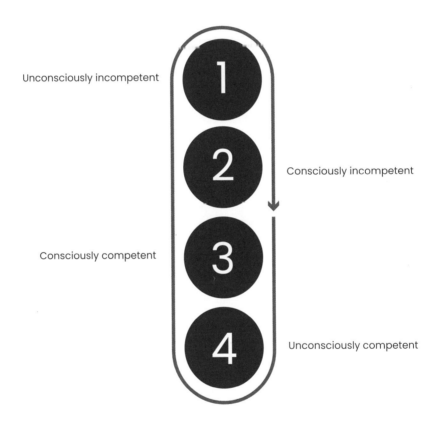

Unconsciously incompetent

Consciously incompetent

Consciously competent

Unconsciously competent

8 RIO SALES COACHING

Successfully selling to any type of customer is not something you learn overnight. It is a process that requires motivation, focus and perseverance. It is also a skill that you develop within a team, as a result of the interaction needed to 'practice'. Sincere feedback from others is crucial to know whether you are on the right track or have missed the ball completely. As with any skill, support from a coach is of great added value. An experienced RIO coach will skillfully guide you through the four stages of development that will ultimately lead you to apply RIO in every human interaction.

Phase 1: The salesperson is not aware that RIO exists and wrongly believes that he sells equally well to every kind of customer. In this phase, sales professionals often divide their customers into the categories 'cool/annoying' or 'easy/tough'.
Phase 2: The sales rep then gets to know RIO and realizes that he has difficulty selling to people who are completely different from him. The sales professional becomes aware of his *stretch customer*.
Phase 3: Through insight, knowledge, practice and adjustment, the salesperson succeeds in adapting himself to the purchasing style of his stretch customer and succeeds in winning deals through conscious focus.
Phase 4: RIO has now become automatic and requires little conscious attention. As a result, every human interaction runs more smoothly.

In this chapter, we describe how sales coaches can provide the most constructive support to salespeople who want to boost their sales results through RIO. We explain what makes RIO sales coaching effective and what the specific focus points and techniques are. We will start this chapter with a clear distinction between personal coaching, commercial coaching and commercial RIO coaching. If you do not have a coaching role within your organization, you can skip this chapter and pick up on the next topic: how to develop yourself into a comprehensive RIO salesperson.

Coaching approaches

INDIVIDUAL COACHING

Personal coaching, or life coaching, is used for matters closely related to a person's private life: struggles in that person's relationship, unprocessed grief, addiction problems or challenges within the family situation. A life coach is then someone who is therapeutically trained and characterized by a pronounced 'pull dynamic'. The coach works almost exclusively by questioning underlying issues with the aim of bringing the coachee to a self-formulated solution to the challenge that he is confronted with. Life coaching is preeminently a method in which reflection and delay are central.

COMMERCIAL COACHING

In commercial coaching, the focus is on increasing professional performance and achieving set goals. Commercial coaching consists of quantitative and qualitative interventions in which figures are used to assess, on the one hand, whether the coachee is sufficiently active and, on the other hand, whether their actions are of a high enough quality. Sufficiently skillful customer interactions will then ensure *predictable revenue*, the dream scenario of every sales manager.

In contrast to personal coaching, commercial coaching is characterized by a pronounced 'push dynamic'. The coach takes the lead during the interventions and offers guidance and advice when problems arise. Commercial coaching is closely related to mentoring in which the coach uses his accumulated knowledge, experience and authority to directly influence the coachee. Commercial coaching is carried out by the coachee's immediate superior at recurring times and according to a fixed pattern. A strict agenda ensures efficiency during the meetings.

COMMERCIAL RIO COACHING

Commercial RIO coaching combines the best of both worlds. It has the goal orientation of commercial coaching and the people orientation of personal coaching. RIO sales coaching is characterized by indirect influence and can therefore best be compared to football coaching, in which the coach would never run onto the pitch to score a goal himself. Before the match, the strategy is discussed, the opponent is analyzed and players are put in charge. During the game, the players use their personal talent and skills to smash the ball into the net, while the coach stands at the touchline with observations, guidelines and encouragement. Afterwards, specific passages of play are reviewed, and the impacts of actions are analyzed. This serves as a feedforward for winning the next match. RIO sales coaching also focuses on continuous improvement and convincing the next customer more efficiently and effectively than the last. In addition, it is hyper-personalized, and personal coaching comes into the picture when people resist and it becomes necessary to work at a deeper level.

RIO sales coaching is a unique process that is characterized by two specific focus points:

» focus on the customer during the sales conversation;
» focus on the coachee during the coaching conversation.

FOCUS ON THE CUSTOMER DURING THE SALES CONVERSATION

Customer experience is king! During the sales conversation, the customer's RIO channel of trust is the focal point! Why is that important? Because an encounter between three people is often a potpourri of behavioral preferences, leading everyone to lose the plot. It is at that moment that the experienced RIO sales coach brings clarity and focuses attention where it should be – on the customer!

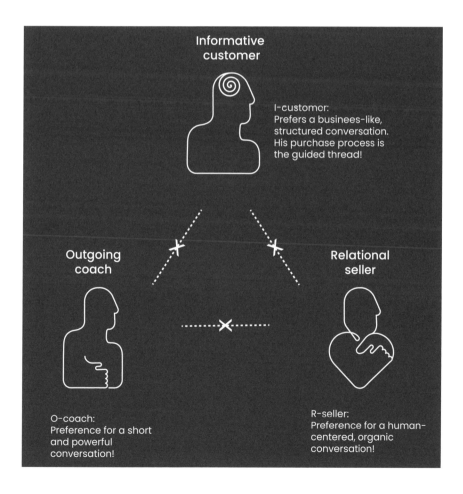

FOCUS ON THE COACHEE DURING THE COACHING CONVERSATION

During RIO sales coaching, it is extremely important to walk the walk. You cannot ask a sales rep to take his customer's personal dynamics into account and then coach them that one size fits all. Just like customers, coachees require a differentiated approach. What motivates one, demotivates another. The hasty conclusion is often that one sales rep 'has it in him' and the other is missing talent. But this conclusion is too simplistic. After all, when you coach without knowledge of RIO, the chances are that you do so from within your primary channel of trust and, as such, it simply fails to resonate with each and every one of your people.

A relational coach will emphasize a consultative approach, customer orientation, service, building long-term relationships and asking many open-ended questions.

'People buy from people who appreciate them.'

An informative coach will focus on the uniformity of each conversation in which the process, preparation, structure, professionalism and professional knowledge are paramount.

'Uniformity in approach and process

makes sales objective and predictable.'

In turn, an outgoing sales coach will steer towards enthusiasm and passion, give tips and tricks for delivering a convincing pitch, work around argumentation, decisive closing and tell you that selling is a battle you must win.

'Selling is always a little war.'

Does it ring a bell? Just as in the sales conversation, coaching's success depends on the alignment between coach and coachee and loses impact when the sales rep does not feel personally addressed. He listens to the tips but fails to apply them because he neither believes in them nor sees himself carrying them out. Here, it is not a lack of general motivation but a mismatch at the RIO level.

Therefore, the conclusion is that the experienced RIO coach excels both in observing sales conversations in a customer-focused way and supporting salespeople during coaching conversations in a sales-focused way. When sales reps are coached based on RIO insights, they become the best-performing version of themselves and an inspiring example for customers and colleagues.

Essential RIO coaching skills

As a RIO coach, you possess a repertoire of skills that you systematically use to develop your coachees. Given your central role, an awareness of your own RIO dynamics is crucial. After all, based on your personal preferences, there are skills that you will naturally be able to use more easily than others. As a RIO coach you need the full repertoire. What skills do you need to develop in order to be a comprehensive coach?

RELATIONAL COACHING SKILLS

» *Be a confidant*: putting yourself 100% at the service of your coachee's growth, without an agenda of your own.
» *Connect*: tuning into the other person with all your senses.
» *Differentiate*: approaching your coachees in a personalized way while respecting their channel of trust.
» *Listen without judgment*: receiving whatever the coachee says, without personal favor or disapproval.
» *Appreciate*: positively supporting your coachee's thoughts, feelings and actions.
» *Inspire*: providing content that visibly enhances your coachee's motivation and insight.
» *Guide*: Guiding the coachee along the path he chooses to walk.

INFORMATIVE COACHING SKILLS

» *Communicate clearly*: creating clarity for the coachee through structured and effective communication.
» *Process-based work*: working according to a logical and predetermined chronology of steps.
» *Observe*: noticing subtle changes in behavior and environmental factors.
» *Substantiate feedback*: linking feedback content to observable events.
» *Objectify*: stripping events of their emotional charge and depicting them objectively.
» *Restructure thinking*: pointing fallacies out to the coachee and offering alternative interpretations.
» *Provide formulas*: providing your coachee with reproducibly effective solutions.

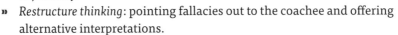

OUTGOING COACHING SKILLS

» *Formulate short-term goals*: making concrete the desired outcome being worked on.
» *Give autonomy*: relying on the coachee's own strength and resilience.
» *Confront*: bringing the coachee into contact with important facts he either does not want to or cannot see.
» *Spar*: quickly exchanging challenging ideas.
» *Think with a solution focus*: making concrete an efficient and effective action to solve a problem.
» *Challenge*: taking the coachee out of his comfort zone.
» *Implement*: carrying out the chosen solution in a planned manner.

Essential RIO coaching techniques

Since the RIO methodology focuses on the interpersonal dynamics between customer and vendor, field coaching is the best format for a coach to contribute to the growth of a coachee. There can be a great deal of discussion about how coordination is to take place, but the proof of the pudding is in the eating. 'Learning by doing' undoubtedly produces the best results.

In field coaching, RIO techniques are used during three key moments:
1. the preparation;
2. the sales conversation;
3. the follow-up conversation.

For the sake of practicality, we will be switching to an action-oriented tone of voice in the material presented below!

THE PREPARATION

The preparatory interview precedes the actual sales conversation. Set aside between thirty and sixty minutes for this. As a sales coach, you generally check the following:
- » What does the coachee know about the client?
- » What does the customer history tell us?
- » Were the questions tailored to the customer and his business?
- » What are the potential pain points at branch, organization and function level?
- » Who are this customer's competitors?
- » What are the important known objections and arguments?
- » What material (iPad, leaflets, etc.) has the coachee brought with them?
- » What is the purpose of the conversation?

Additionally, as a RIO sales coach you will focus on the following elements:
1. your coachee's motivation;
2. feedforward;
3. RIO exercise.

MOTIVATION

'Well done is better than well said.'

– BENJAMIN FRANKLIN, FOUNDING FATHER
OF THE UNITED STATES OF AMERICA

During the preparatory interview it is especially important to motivate your coachee. After all, growth and behavioral change are driven by 'hunger'. What motivates someone is very closely related to his channel of trust. Here is an overview of what motivates and demotivates the different RIO types.

RELATIONAL SELLERS are motivated by:	RELATIONAL SELLERS are demotivated by::
• Achieving goals together • Good atmosphere at work • Learning (about themselves) • Personal appreciation • Supporting others in achieving their goals • Being passionate in their work • Freedom to do things differently • Depth and sensitivity in the interlocutor	• Competitive committees • No personal appreciation • Superficiality • No room for expressing feelings • Being treated like everyone else • Being required to do something • Bad atmosphere • Too many tasks and responsibilities
INFORMATIVE SELLERS are motivated by:	INFORMATIVE SELLERS are demotivated by:
• Clear expectations and rules of play • Clear bonus system • Smart strategies • Correct agreements • Substantiated feedback • Effectiveness with limited resources • Business-like interaction with each other • Automation and standardization • Order and cleanliness	• Chaos • Unclear expectations • Changing strategies • Unfulfilled agreements • Stupid management decisions • Constantly changing strategy • Familiar interaction • Unfinished tasks • No appreciation for quality
OUTGOING SELLERS are motivated by:	OUTGOING SELLERS are demotivated by:
• Commission • Personal recognition • Challenging but achievable goals • Efficient and effective solutions • Decisive people • Quick action • Fair feedback • Multitude of stimulating tasks • Innovation • Enthusiasm • Impactful projects	• Negativity • Lack of reward • Dishonesty • No clear and achievable goals • Wasting time, things dragging on • Too many formalities • Having no impact or perspective • Dull, repetitive tasks • Personal criticism • Weak leadership

FEEDFORWARD

Feed*forward* is an exceptionally valuable technique during the preparation phase. The difference from feed*back* is fundamental. Rather than look back at a situation in the past you instead focus on the future. Feedforward's positive effects are:

» You have an impact on the future, not on the past. People have the feeling of control, while feedback often feels like it is a process to be endured.

» The focus is on positive desired behavior. Unlike in feedback with negative behavior, feedforward identifies and reinforces the positive.

» It gives the RIO coach insight into his coachee's personal potential. With feedforward you show that you believe in your coachee's potential, which inspires self-confidence.

Feedforward is important at both the coachee and client level.

• Feedforward at the coachee level

You start with feedforward on a personal level. This requires insight into your coachee's personal RIO sequence and the associated strengths and pitfalls. What is the employee's RIO profile and what does that mean for the course of the conversation?

EXAMPLE 1

You are going to speak with a relational coachee. Knowing that it is often a challenge for him to lead and close in a positive way, you can ask the following questions to activate his awareness of this:

» Looking ahead, how will your relational channel of trust help you make this conversation a success?

» How can your relational channel cause problems?

» How would you like to open this conversation?

» How are you going to maintain the balance between push and pull?

» What questions are you going to ask to clarify the customer's current challenges?

» What closing questions could you ask at the end of the conversation?

» How can we be sure that there is commitment from the customer afterwards?

EXAMPLE 2

You are going to speak with an informative coachee. Knowing that connection and personalized value creation are often challenging for him, you can ask the following questions in order to broaden those skills:

» Looking ahead, how will your informative channel of trust help you make this conversation a success?
» How can your informative channel cause problems?
» How can you start with a professional but inviting opener?
» How are you going to maintain the balance between push and pull?
» Which information is crucial when presenting your offer?
» How do you want to pin down the *next step* at the end of a conversation?

EXAMPLE 3

You are going to speak with an outgoing coachee. Knowing that he often struggles with active listening and having patience, you can ask the following questions to bring that to his attention:

» Looking ahead, how will your outgoing channel of trust help you make this conversation a success?
» How can your outgoing channel cause problems?
» What questions are you going to ask to find out what is important to this customer?
» What reformulating sentence can you use?
» What check can you build in to see whether you went for a 'quick win' or a long-term solution?
» How can you verify whether the customer is experiencing a win-win at the end of the call?

An important point is that consciousness- and focus-inspiring feedforward can also be used with coachees who have not identified their channel of trust. As a coach, you must then work 'implicitly' with RIO and determine the correct focus by asking questions, while leaving out the 'explicit' designation of R, I or O.

- **Feedforward at the customer level**

The coachee will use the RIO method during the conversation. In order to successfully complete this process, preparation at the RIO level is necessary. Important here are:

- » Knowledge of the differentiated RIO conversation trajectories.
- » Insight into the customer/prospect's RIO profile. A proactive assessment of the client based on available information is ideal.
- » Customer behavior is key. With RIO, the focus is always on the customer's needs. His behavior and reactions always indicate whether or not the salesperson is providing him with what he needs. During the preparatory interview, you and your coachee should go through the different RIO conversations that apply. Indicate what is essential for this type of client. In this way, it is neither about your preference as a coach nor about the coachee's preference, but instead about the client's channel of trust. The client's profile determines the focus.

As a coach, you can ask the following questions in the interest of the RIO connection:

1 The customer is an R
- » How are you going to build the conversation, knowing the prospect is an R?
- » What soft opener are you going to use to put this customer at ease?
- » What do you know about this client personally?
- » What customer-focused closing phrase would you like to use later?

2 The customer is an I
- » How are you going to build the conversation knowing the prospect is an I?
- » What figures are you going to use in your argument?
- » Shall we go over the standard presentation together one last time?
- » What are the advantages and disadvantages of our offer compared to our competitor's?

3 The customer is an O
- » How are you going to build the conversation knowing that the prospect is probably an O?
- » What does your pitch look like?
- » What challenging questions can you ask this customer?
- » What concrete proposal can you make at the end of this conversation?

RIO STRETCH EXERCISE
With certain customers things just never quite seem to work. This will also come up during preparation. The coachee dreads the conversation and refers

to an 'exceptionally difficult' customer. That is his stretch client. Research shows that the last letter in our RIO sequence requires the largest stretch, although we have all three of the dynamics within ourselves. The last letter in our sequence is the dynamic that we have disregarded. As a result, it is also underdeveloped. In chapter 10 we will go into more detail. If, as a coach, you notice that a coachee has an underdeveloped RIO segment, you can draw his attention to these dynamics during preparation so that they will be more present during the conversation.

EXAMPLE

Take a coachee with an ORI profile who will soon have to speak with an exceedingly informative client. The informative channel comes last for this coachee, which means that structure, preparation, details and numerical argumentation are major challenges for him. Ask the coachee if there is a situation in which he finds it easy to be well prepared. Maybe he is very protective as a father and makes sure that everything is well planned in the family. Get him to think of a situation like this. You can ask the following questions so that he becomes more aware of the informative channel within himself:

- » What business are you looking for?
- » So how do you keep track of everything?
- » Then why is that so important?
- » So, what details matter?
- » So, how do you feel?
- » Where is that energy exactly?
- » Is that easy for you to reach now?

In doing so, you, as the RIO coach, bring the informative dynamic more to the fore and indicate that he will be able to appeal to this dynamic during the conversation with his client. The new awareness that he carries the informative channel within himself provides a fundamentally different starting position. The coachee will no longer mentally remove himself from the conversation, but instead will make the connection because he recognizes and appreciates the dynamic within himself. That creates connection.

COACHING DURING THE SALES CONVERSATION

FORMS

There are three didactic conversation forms that you can choose as a RIO coach. Though they offer different learning opportunities, each of the three are valuable.

1   The observation conversation

As coach/manager, you lead the sales conversation. The coachee has the opportunity to follow, observe, take notes and capture in a passive role. The coachee is introduced as a colleague. For informative and relational coachees, this first form is a safe way to get acquainted with you as a coach. Informative people are fond of learning through observation. After the conversation, they like to analyze what happened. In this way, they also know what is expected of them. Relational coaches also find observation interviews a comfortable start to coaching. They like to get a sense of your sales style and how they can attune to it.

2   The team conversation

This is a conversation in which both coach and coachee take the floor. The customer gets, as it were, 'two for the price of one'. Working synergistically, coach and coachee complement each other. As a coach, the challenge here is then to give structured feedback afterwards, given that you were personally involved in the conversation. You can agree in advance about who will be 'in the lead' during the conversation. For informative coachees this format is a challenge. It feels very much all over the place. Moreover, the roles are unclear. Unless there are two additional areas of expertise, this is difficult. This format can also be a challenge for outgoing coachees. Given their strong opinions and energy, this could give a customer a two-against-one feeling. Relational coachees love this format because it is the most organic form of conversation and gives them a strong feeling of being and working together.

3   The do-it-yourself conversation

Here, the coachee conducts the conversation and the coach follows without interfering. The coach introduces himself as a 'colleague in training' and then assumes a passive role, no matter how the conversation goes! It is best not to do this kind of conversation with clients that risk a large potential loss. What is important to know about this conversation format is that informative coachees tend to underperform. Assessment creates negative stress. A timely and regularly scheduled interview ensures that the informative coachee feels safer over time. Outgoing coachees, on the other hand, like to put their best foot forward at the moment of truth, which can also give you a distorted picture. As a coach, be aware of this. After DIY conversations, it is common to hear a statement such as: 'I usually do that completely differently!' Question this claim with interest but know that coachees will usually make more or less the same mistakes as when you are not there.

CUSTOMER BEHAVIOR IS KEY!

As indicated at the beginning of this chapter, customer satisfaction is the benchmark for measuring the quality of the conversation. A visibly committed customer is the precursor to the kind of sustainable purchase that this book is all about. The following table contains parameters that make it easy to check whether the connection between customer and seller is being maintained. In reality, connection loss looks different for each RIO customer type, but the impact remains the same: the chance of a successful conclusion diminishes noticeably.

- **Visible signs of a strong connection with relational customers**

A smooth dialogue is always a good sign from relational customers. They talk, laugh and listen. The energy flows from one person to another. The connection is palpable.

Opening	Presentation	Engagement
• Broad smiles • Ask how you're feeling • Enthusiasm • Chat about personal matters	• Listen attentively and make friendly eye contact • Approving sounds and nods • Maintain dialogue throughout • Link to personal situation	• Ask for help with decision-making • Want you to be the contact person after the decision • Chat afterwards on a personal level

- **Visible signs of connection loss with relational clients**

Relational customers are very good at making it look as if there is still a connection. Though they are already emotionally disconnected, they will seemingly continue to listen, nod and even smile kindly. They are, however, not really recording information anymore. They patiently sit out the conversation and dodge the engagement question with a vague excuse such as 'I have to discuss this again at home.'

Opening	Presentation	Engagement
• Become quieter • Active participation in the conversation decreases • Constantly smile, nod and agree with you	• Distracted • Attention on other people • Passively present	• Postpone • Hide behind another person • Say they still need to think it over

Hopefully, the coach and coachee are sufficiently alert to notice the connection loss and use connection-repairing questions to turn the tide. This creates new space and gives the relational customer oxygen to get back into the conversation. The connection can be restored by means of open-ended questions that gauge the customer's feelings:

» What's your feeling so far?
» I've told you a lot. How are you finding it?
» It's probably a great deal of information. How does it seem to you?
» Tell me, what's really important to you personally?

- **Visible signs of a strong connection with informative customers**

For informative customers, the 'connection' is mainly on an intellectual level. It manifests itself in a conversation in which both parties are visibly involved and learn from each other's expertise. What starts as a business conversation gradually evolves into a dialogue in which personal matters are also shared.

Opening	Presentation	Engagement
• Polite attentive look • Customer gives the seller space to introduce their organization • Customer asks interested questions during the opening phase	• Make notes during the presentation • Look that conveys 'processing information' • Interested questions • Customer makes valuable contributions	• Customer wants to jointly consider • Customer wants to have a thorough look at the contract • Asks about the process after purchase • Asks about the timing

- **Visible signs of connection loss with informative customers**

A business-like, withdrawn attitude is not a sign of connection loss from informative customers. It indicates that they are absorbing and processing the information, which is a good signal. I-customers disconnect at ambiguity, familiarity and emotional statements. This becomes visible when they begin to question the salesperson's expertise.

Opening	Presentation	Engagement
• Closed position • Deep frown • Arrogance • What exactly is this about? • Short answers, if any	• Discussion of content • Question things • Challenge data • Psychological war	• Say they still want to make another thorough comparison • Set negative points in the spotlight

Here, too, the coachee can use connection-repairing questions to turn the tide. To do so, it is important to establish where clarity and credibility have been lost. This can be done using illuminating questions:

» I notice I'm not being 100% clear. What questions do you have exactly?
» Which area would you like to explore in more detail?
» Does this match up with what you already knew about the subject?

- **Visible signs of a strong connection with outgoing customers**

Outgoing customers are very expressive. When there is a strong connection, the conversation unfolds with a clear *oomph* to it. Sparring goes firmly but respectfully, the dialogue goes back and forth, and parties come to a decision quickly.

Opening	Presentation	Engagement
• Do not mince words • Captivated listening and confirmation • Clear about expectations • Say what they are looking for	• Affirmative language 'wow, super, oh I'm sure' • Sparring • Enthusiastic • Move towards close	• Close on their own • Ask about the 'next step' • Express positive feelings about decision

- **Visible signs of connection loss with outgoing clients**

Although outgoing clients are sometimes seen as extremely challenging, they are the easiest to read. What you see is what you get. Either there is a match or there is not. Their reactions are markedly negative or positive. When a connection is lost it is clearly stated. The biggest triggers are a slow pace, insufficiently strong offer and dishonesty.

Opening	Presentation	Engagement
• Restless posture • Checks watch • Challenging comments • Takes the upper hand	• Constantly interrupting • Looking tough in silence • Spouting excessive arguments • Distracted	• Playing games • Simply says that it is too expensive • Ends conversation

Once again, the coachee can make use of connection-repairing questions when he loses the customer's attention. To do this, it is important to quicken the pace of the conversation and openly state what is happening:

» I can see the presentation doesn't interest you much. How would you approach this?
» You know best what you need, tell me...
» I see you disagree with me.

It is possible to reconnect with RIO customers at any time. It is, therefore, up to you as a coach to help your coachee to do so.

OBSERVATION AND NOTATION IN RIO SALES CONVERSATIONS

Observing, listening and noting structured feedback all at the same time: field discussions are also a challenge for the RIO coach. It is certainly not passively reclining. Only through well-founded feedback can you achieve a change in behavior.

We therefore strongly recommend using a structured document during observation. You can download the RIO-CSS document at www.blinc.be/nl/mensen-raken-klanten-maken. CSS stands for 'Continue - Start - Stop'.
For each stage of the sales conversation, the most important skills are listed by customer type. During the observation, you then write down what the coachee did and said as literally as possible, and divide this into three categories:
» *Continue*: Keep doing this. What you did or said here had a positive impact on the process.
» *Start*: This was missing. Build it in next time to positively influence the customer.
» *Stop*: This action or statement was counterproductive. Avoid them in all subsequent conversations.

	Continue	Start	Stop
Include			
• Clear agenda-setting and timing			
• Your background			
• Your company's structure			
• Business-like attitude			

On the CSS (Continue – Start – Stop) document, you could use suitable emoticons. They allow you to display the client's state of mind.

It is important to underline that there should be three specific CSS documents, one for each of the customer types. As a RIO sales coach, it is therefore crucial to make a correct assessment of the customer and note your feedback on the correct document.

The importance of feedback

CATEGORIES OF FEEDBACK

Feedback, the breakfast of every champion and your coachee's fuel for behavioral change. Unlike the previous phases, the focus is now on the coachee's channel of trust. It is therefore important to distinguish between the content of the feedback, which is based on the customer's channel of trust, and the form, which is tailored to the coachee.

The basis for the feedback conversation is your notes on the CSS document. We identify three types of observation based on the impact they have on the coachee and suggest a specific way to share them with the coachee.

NEUTRAL OBSERVATIONS

Neutral observations are not that sensitive and will be accepted by the coachee without any problem. You can then share them with your coachee without much fuss. For example: 'You made a clicking sound with your ballpoint pen and that distracted the client.'

IMPORTANT OBSERVATIONS

Important observations are moderately sensitive and the form in which the feedback is delivered determines whether the coachee will accept or reject it. It is best to use a professional feedback model such as DESC.

Describe: describe the exact behavior you observed. 'Halfway through the conversation, you said the cost of your machine is about 100k.'

Express: share the impact this behavior had on the customer. 'The informative customer was shocked by that remark and stayed silent from that moment on...'

Suggest: suggest alternative behavior. 'In the case of an informative customer, it's best to check whether your price is in line with his expectations.'

Commit: check to see if the coachee wants to commit to this. 'Do you see yourself doing that at your next meeting with an informative client?'

SENSITIVE OBSERVATIONS

Sensitive observations are extremely delicate because they are linked to the person's core beliefs. There is a real chance that this feedback will generate resistance, which makes a more thorough coaching approach such as GROW necessary. We will apply the GROW model to a situation in which an outgoing sales rep is not listening enough to a relational client.

- **Step 1. Goal (objective)**

The first step of the GROW coaching model is to determine the goal, both for the longer term and for the short term. The objective is often linked to an observation made during field coaching. Example questions for determining the objective:
  - » 'What's important to you in terms of [theme]?'
  - » 'What is/was your intention?'

Example: I found that you were talking 80% of the time and listening 20%. What's the reason you did that?

- **Step 2. Reality (actual situation)**

The second step is to explore the current situation. The role of the coach is to stimulate the coachee to self-evaluate and analyze concrete examples. Example questions for exploring the actual situation:
  - » 'What was the result of that?'
  - » 'What went wrong then?'

Example: Did you see how the customer reacted to that? Was that the effect you intended?

- **Step 3. Options (explore options)**

The aim of the third step in the GROW coaching model is to generate ideas that can contribute to solving the problem. Example questions for generating options:
  - » 'What else could you do?'
  - » 'What are the pros and cons of this option?'

Example: How can you encourage yourself to listen more to the customer?

- **Step 4. Will (motivation, action plan, conclusion)**

The fourth and final step is to arrive at a solution to which the coachee is committed. Example questions for generating concrete action are:

» 'What's the first concrete step you can take right now?'
» 'How motivated are you to pursue this option?'

Example: If you say that you listen better when you take more notes, can I assume you'll bring a notebook next time? How are you going to take notes during the conversation this afternoon?

Feedback tips tailored to RIO coachees

Receiving feedback is a challenge for many people. With regard to RIO, we have noted the following:

1 Outgoing types deal well with feedback from people they respect. If comments are shared honestly and in person, you rise in their esteem as a coach. They will go on the defensive if they think the feedback is unfair. They have a strong sense of justice. At the same time, the end justifies the means, which makes it difficult to give points of improvements when they close the deal despite a bad conversation.

2 Relational types are especially afraid that the personal relationship will suffer because of their diminished professional performance. Feedback comes in as a personal attack and they feel rejected. It is therefore crucial to make the personal connection tangible during a feedback interview. Be careful with the famous 'sandwich technique'. When the point of improvement is inserted between two compliments, it is often no longer clear that change is actually expected.

3 Informative types have great difficulty with unclear or emotional feedback. Statements such as 'I didn't have a good feeling about this conversation' should absolutely be avoided. When feedback is clear, substantiated and structured, they are happy to accept it. They do, however, need time to process the incoming information. Defining action points or new goals is best done at a later moment.

The following feedback tips ensure that your coachee's channel of trust remains open during the feedback conversation. Trust ensures that a coachee really listens, instead of focusing his attention on replying from a place of resistance. Ask for your coachee's opinion after every form of feedback.

RELATIONAL SELLERS
Feedback dos

- Introduce your feedback with personal appreciation
- Indicate the impact of his behavior on others
- Briefly state what behavior you wish to see
- Provide room for a response and show understanding of good intentions
- Leave room for his own initiative
- Close positively and with appreciation

RELATIONAL SELLERS
Feedback don'ts

- Immediately get to the essence of your feedback
- Make the problem a big deal
- Provide no room for a response
- Minimize his response
- Provide a detailed explanation of the solution
- Cool and business-like closure

INFORMATIVE SELLERS
Feedback dos

- Choose an appropriate place and time
- Identify the professional relevance of your feedback
- Be specific, factual, objective and concrete
- Provide a proven solution and mention your source
- Leave room for a reaction, remain steadfast
- Clarify the basis of logical cause-and-effect reasoning

INFORMATIVE SELLERS
Feedback don'ts

- Provide no framework
- Fail to appreciate qualitative intention and professionalism
- Fail to recognize personal efforts
- Offer vague feedback, give little factual feedback
- Speak from your feelings
- Deprive them of time to think

OUTGOING SELLERS
Feedback dos

- Deliver feedback with strength and self-assurance
- Provide feedback according to the facts
- Share the purpose and practical usefulness of your feedback
- Offer short guidelines and autonomy
- Be clear, but leave room for a reaction
- Do not emphasize the problem as much as the quick solution

OUTGOING SELLERS
Feedback don'ts

- Express yourself in soft and vague terms
- Take too long to reach the essence (if at all)
- Only raise the problem and not offer a solution
- Speak from your feelings
- Leave no room for reaction
- Demand that the coachee calm down
- Get stuck in negative feedback

Personal check-up as a RIO sales coach

We will conclude this chapter with some tips for monitoring your impact as a RIO sales coach. Even though, as a sales coach, we all want people to make instant behavioral changes and their results to skyrocket, the effect of RIO sales coaching visibly unfolds in four phases:

1 The coachee attentively listens and enthusiastically takes up the recommendations.
2 During a subsequent coaching interview, he applies the matters discussed.
3 He applies the techniques, even when you are not present.
4 The coachee systematically achieves better sales results.

If we really want to support our coachees in altering their behavior, it is then important to keep the formula for behavioral change in mind:

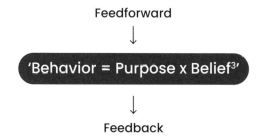

A coachee will change his behavior when he is motivated and believes the new habits received through feedback and feedforward are effective and realistic and come from a coach who, in turn, believes in him.

Although this formula may seem simple, it challenges you to think critically about the following questions after each coaching session.

1 Does my coachee have a goal that motivates him/her?
2 Does he believe in the effectiveness of the desired behavior?
3 Does he see himself doing it?
4 Do I believe in the coachee and will I invest in continuous feedback?

It is only when you can formulate a convincing answer to each of these questions that there is a real chance your coachee will make progress... in baby steps.

We often see coaches setting expectations that are too high, in spite of knowing that changing ingrained behavior is incredibly difficult. It requires openness, motivation, repetition and support. Something that might seem miniscule is actually a huge shift. When a relational coachee succeeds in limiting the needs analysis to three questions instead of 10 for an outgoing client, it deserves a party! Every extra minute that an outgoing sales rep listens is admiration-worthy and every personal fact that an informative coachee shares with his client is a step forward. So be proud and validate every baby step that coachees take. People do not change simply like that; the fact that coachees do so in your presence is an honor and a privilege.

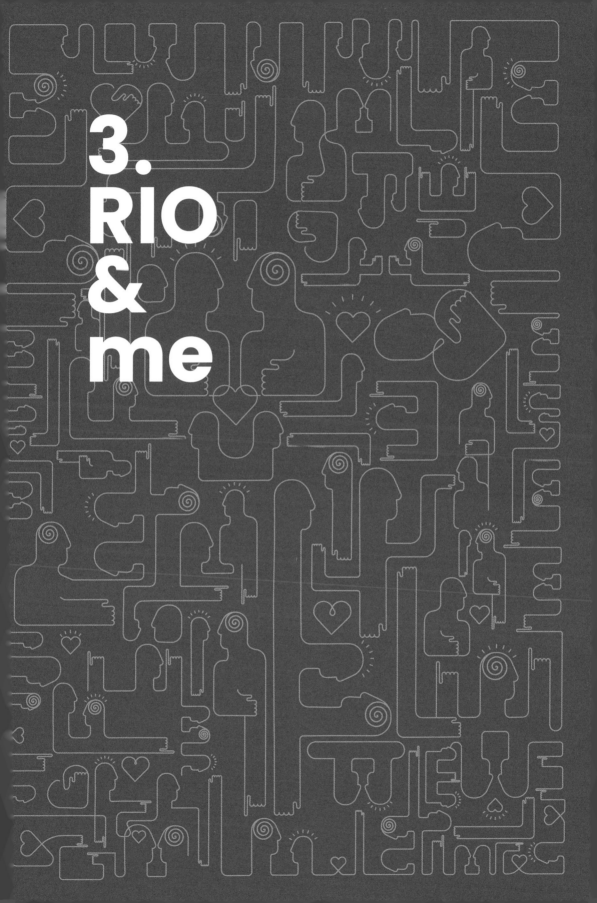

3.
RIO
&
me

*How do I recognize
my channel
of trust?*

———

*How do I become
a comprehensive
RIO salesperson?*

Although RIO is a pragmatic model for looking at customers, we have found that, in the first instance, it is a challenge for sales professionals to identify their own preferred channel. This chapter therefore focuses on practical tools that help with self-typing. We present both personal and professional RIO passports that home in on typical behavior, strengths and pitfalls within a specific context. The purpose of these tools is to provide concrete support in your self-reflection. The invitation is to dare to feel, think and 'come back down' as you absorb this information. Only you can best assess what your most common behavior is at the moment a situation feels exciting. Doubt is certainly normal, and we are happy to answer the most frequently asked questions about self-typing later in this chapter. Use all of the information in this book to get to know yourself better in both commercial and non-commercial situations. Talk to people you trust about your RIO channel and consider their feedback. If you are still in doubt after these steps, we offer you a code for an online test. Combining all of these clues will lead you to valuable insights about yourself and the behavioral patterns you primarily use at work and in your life. The goal is not characterization but an awareness of your talents and opportunities for growth.

We will start with the three personal RIO passports, real stories of real people. Sit back, relax and enjoy the ride!

ROI passport

> Name: Dirk Valgaeren
> Age: 48 years
> Birthplace: Winch, Belgium
> Profession: Commercial trainer & coach
> RIO sequence: ROI

——————

GENERAL:
My name is Dirk Valgaeren and I prefer the relational channel of trust. People in my environment see me as an open, accessible and gentle person who, when necessary, can win people over with an outgoing and solution-focused dynamic. When I think about it, that also matches how I feel about myself.

I thrive when the people around me are doing well and I take my time to listen when I feel that something is not right.

___

ROI AS CUSTOMER:

When I think about it, if I am the customer, it is less about what the salesperson says than about the way the conversation goes. What is super important is that I get the chance to explain exactly what I want to achieve, what I am looking for and why it is important, in such a way that I get the feeling that I am being 'advised'. I really want to take my time to make sure that I have explained things well.

Selling to me is therefore both easy and difficult: if the seller can earn my trust that I am being correctly advised (and knows that I can sense fake behavior right away), I can make a quick decision without comparing or even looking at – let alone negotiating – the price. If I feel the opposite, I am still going to stay friendly until a point when I can come out feisty, saying something like: 'And how do you know if everything you're telling me is even relevant to me?'.

___

ROI AS A SALESPERSON:

I do very well in consultative sales within large organizations, where you can build a long-term relationship with people and achieve success by following the right growth path based on a profound understanding of the organization.

I take a lot of time to get to know the organization and the people behind it thoroughly. The advantage is that I can work towards bigger deals, but the disadvantage is that I find it difficult to close something quickly due to figures.

My biggest challenge is when I do not feel respected by my clients as a human being because they instead want to be commercially active in a different dynamic. For example, I once simply passed a large dossier on to one of my colleagues because the collaboration was not 'real'. Many of my colleagues (apart from the one who got the deal thrown in his lap) told me I was 'foolish' to miss out on so much commission because of a feeling, but yes, it was deep.

ROI CONTEXT-DEPENDENT BEHAVIOR:

I think my behavior varies little across contexts. My sense of trust in some-one and my lower focus on preparation can sometimes project an image of 'not being involved enough' in certain spheres (for example, when planning a holiday, I trust my wife to take care of that, which can sometimes seem like a lack of involvement), and an excessive longing for the people around me to feel good sometimes drives my children a little mad when I speak about how they feel…

IOR passport

Name: Vincent Diercxsens
Age: 55 years
Birthplace: Wilrijk, Belgium
Profession: Business coach
RIO sequence: IOR

GENERAL:

My name is Vincent Diercxsens and I prefer the informative and outgoing channels. Both are present in a reasonably balanced way. I am very analytical, and in decisions I always take 'calculated risks' based on as many objective facts as possible. I need to be able to compare objectively, and I can usually map out the possible consequences of a decision very quickly. I like figures and I make eager use of them to map out the return on investment of solu-tions in advance.

I am also a driven person, action-oriented, 'I like to win'. I enjoy working in a team where the feelings of solidarity and teamplay stimulate me incredibly. I like to take the lead in getting things 'moving' and enthusiasm always has to be expressed through an 'energetic approach'.

IOR AS CUSTOMER:

As a client, I usually know very well in advance what the problem is and what solutions I am looking for. I therefore expect the supplier to be able to quickly demonstrate the right solution to me using his expertise.

Still, I will not just trust the seller, and I won't rely on my intuition either; I will dig deeper there to make sure that what the seller is offering me is the right solution. I will compare solutions with others, and never buy immediately and impulsively.

I expect the seller to have a good command of his subject matter and to know my file well and to have analyzed it beforehand. He must be able to answer my questions and do so in a coherent way. He will quickly lose credibility if he cannot.

___

IOR AS A SALESPERSON:

As a salesperson, I have always chosen to work for companies that sold products with a high added value. If you can convince people based on an objective proposition, with high added value, then the choice for the customer will be logical and not dependent on emotional aspects. I have therefore had a very difficult time with customers who made their choices based on purely relational motivations, without looking at the impact of their choices on their business.

___

IOR CONTEXT-DEPENDENT BEHAVIOUR:

My behavior at work is different than at home. At work I am professional and not inclined to open myself up to situations that are personal or from my private life. People do not really get a 'warm' feeling from me, but rather an efficient and goal-oriented impression.

At home I show more of myself. Home is also the place where I open my heart to others, sympathize with them very emotionally and can be a 'softy'. Family experiences touch me deeply and I am someone who lives 300% for his family.

ORI passport

Name: Koen Vandendriessche
Age: 41 years
Place of birth: Izegem, Belgium
Profession: Sales manager
RIO sequence: ORI

GENERAL:

My name is Koen Vandendriessche and I am sure that my channel of trust
is the outgoing channel. When I got the result for the first time, this was of
course no surprise. I have known for a long time that I am quite extroverted,
very results-oriented and also enjoy the impact I have on an organization or a
team. I prefer to be busy making changes, motivating people to get involved
in those changes, and trying out and implementing new initiatives.

'Standing still is going backwards', 'Do the right things rather than do things
right'... statements I have certainly made before.

Meeting deadlines is a nice challenge for me, but when it comes to figure
analysis or even just purely administrative tasks, I find it a little less cool.

ORI AS CUSTOMER:

As a customer, I very often get uncomfortable when the salesperson starts
comparing prices for me, setting benchmarks and beating around the bush
for ages when it comes to the service or product. I can go without coffee during the conversation, but I do want a solution to my need as soon as possible.

In these modern times, I will try new digital sales solutions, but often notice
that I pick up the phone afterwards to arrange things quickly from a distance.

I will set up an appointment online, but when I see that the timeslot is set for
an hour, I will then pick up the phone or e-mail again to arrange things. If,
during an e-mail exchange, a salesperson suddenly suggests we do a quick
video call, I will immediately grab the opportunity.

ORI AS A SALESPERSON:

As a salesman I once received a sales dossier with nice calculations in which the ROI was shown, prices were compared ... after two months I had completely changed it myself. Benefits were shown, strong words were used, a nice value proposition worked out ... really tailored to my needs. Well, I did not use them a whole lot, because in the end I chose to convince the customer through the conversation, the interaction, the verbal power.... in other words, to make the purchase happen through me. Often, I have also had a click with purchasers where things had to move quickly, and they did not even ask for a single quote and immediately made their decision after that. Of course, it has also happened that I have had a buyer who was more of an accountant and this was often energy-consuming for me ... especially when that person asked me to compare his current situation with my solution, and then also asked for 10 different offers according to different payment terms, volumes, duration of the contract, etc.

ORI CONTEXT-DEPENDENT BEHAVIOR:

I do not really adjust my behavior. I would much rather stay authentic. What you see is what you get... People around me always know what they will get from me. Usually I am also the person in the funny situations or jokes.

And when an event or weekend is organized with friends, I am also the person who gets thing started, arranges and communicates everything.

Where I do often hold up a mirror to myself is when I have to recruit people for my team. I try as much as possible to find a different channel of trust so as to strengthen my team.

Last year I was looking for a new right hand to support sales. The choice finally fell on the channel where I get little energy from and where I also dare to procrastinate... You have two guesses as to which one that was...

Psycho-commercial profiles

Some people find it easier not to look at private and professional contexts, but instead only at their own behavior within their sales role. What follows are the six psycho-commercial profiles, descriptions of the RIO sales types along with their natural commercial focus. The goal is identical to that of the passports: offering you extra support in achieving commercial self-knowledge.

——

PSYCHO-COMMERCIAL PROFILE OF THE RIO SELLER

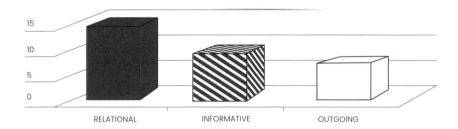

COMMERCIAL FOCUS AND DYNAMICS

For you, the relationship with the customer is central in sales. You do not approach prospects and customers with the aim of selling, but instead with a desire to help and advise them. You listen thoroughly to their needs and suggest the possible solutions you can offer. You give your customer the information he needs and then time to think. People appreciate that you are not a smooth or pushy salesperson, but that you really think along with them and with their needs in mind. You have a natural talent for empathizing with customers and engaging with them because you radiate trust and calm.

PROFESSIONAL VALUES AND STANDARDS

- Customer satisfaction
- Listening skills
- Openness
- Diplomacy

- Transparency
- Win-win
- Modesty
- Sensitivity

CUSTOMER RELATIONS

Favorite customer

Hospitable customers who are willing to speak openly about their desires and then listen to your advice.

Stretch customer

Customers who urge you to get to the point and challenge you to convince them of the profitability of your solution.

THE RIO SELLER'S COMMERCIAL MOTTO:

Every customer likes to receive personalized advice from a humble expert who knows his trade.

PSYCHO-COMMERCIAL PROFILE OF THE ROI SELLER

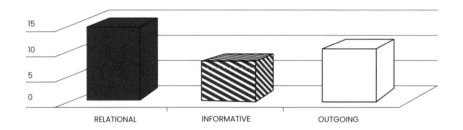

COMMERCIAL FOCUS AND DYNAMICS

For you, too, the relationship with the customer is central in sales. You believe 100% in the added value you can offer. You succeed in uncovering your customer and prospect's needs and convincing them of the appropriate solution. You give your customers the information they need and guide them in a friendly but decisive way towards the right decision. People appreciate that you are not a slick salesman, but that you actively guide them according to their needs. You have a natural talent for getting customers excited and drawing them into a positive story that makes them feel good about themselves.

PROFESSIONAL VALUES AND STANDARDS

- Customer-centric
- Listening skills
- Tailored advice
- Transferring positive energy to the customer

- Just
- Win-win
- Quick transitions based on the needs of the client
- Works with reference clients

Favorite customer	Stretch customer
Enthusiastic customers who are willing to speak openly about their desires and needs after which, based on an energetic dialogue, they make a decision and choose your solution.	Customers who indicate that they want to gather more information and, based on an objective analysis of different parties, will make a decision within an unspecified time frame.

THE ROI SELLER'S COMMERCIAL MOTTO:

A customer wants to be guided, in a way that is personal and action-oriented, towards the best solution to their problem.

PSYCHO-COMMERCIAL PROFILE OF THE IRO-SELLER

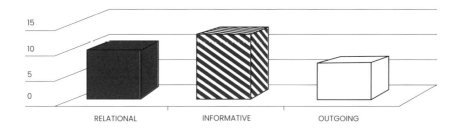

RELATIONAL   INFORMATIVE   OUTGOING

COMMERCIAL FOCUS AND DYNAMICS

You sell with knowledge and insight into your customer's market. You are always well prepared, and you understand your customer's situation. You manage to convince customers to opt for long-term collaboration using well-founded and quantitative arguments. Your intrinsic curiosity enables you to get to the heart of the matter. You ask intelligent questions so that the customer recognizes that you know his business well and that creates trust. You want to achieve your objective in a strategic way but always with respect for the customer. Customers appreciate that they are given space and time to reflect in order to decide. You strive for a balanced win-win situation.

PROFESSIONAL VALUES AND STANDARDS

- Intelligent questioning
- Market knowledge
- Advise clients with quantitative arguments
- Sharp observer

- Body language
- Sharpness
- Allow the customer to think
- Structural solutions for the customer

CUSTOMER RELATIONS

Favorite customer

Intelligent customers who make an informed decision based on well-founded reasoning. Customers who have an eye for the return on investment and objectively choose the best party.

Stretch customer

Emotional customers who jump from one topic to the next and are not interested in substantiated arguments. Knowledgeable and blunt customers who think they do not need information..

THE IRO SALESPERSON'S COMMERCIAL MOTTO:

If I can objectively demonstrate the added value of my service/product for this client and he understands that, then my client will opt for a partnership.

PSYCHO-COMMERCIAL PROFILE OF THE IOR SELLER

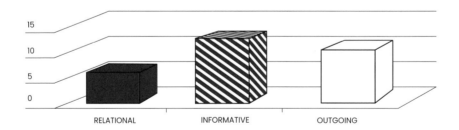

COMMERCIAL FOCUS AND DYNAMICS

You are a smart salesperson who strives to achieve commercial objectives in a structured and well-considered way. You put a great deal of energy into fine-tuning your sales story. You succeed in convincing customers that your solution will provide the highest return on investment by means of well-founded and quantitative arguments. You work systematically and have iron discipline. You are not distracted by emotions, neither your own nor the customer's. Sales is a strategic game and knowledge is power. You pursue challenging objectives and want to achieve them based on perseverance and a defined plan of action.

PROFESSIONAL VALUES AND STANDARDS

- Smart sales process
- Strategic insight
- Perseverance
- Structured

- Strong preparation
- Professional
- Perception is reality
- Powerful orator

CUSTOMER RELATIONS

Favorite customer

High level customers who are convinced by strongly substantiated arguments that demonstrate market and professional knowledge. Clients who want to shift gears quickly and do not allow themselves to be distracted by emotions.

Stretch customer

Slow, dreamy customers who are unfamiliar with the files. Clients who keep going back on previous agreements.

THE IOR SALESMAN'S COMMERCIAL MOTTO:

Thanks to my professional and resolute manner, I convince customers of my expertise. Using clear and well-founded arguments, I succeed in turning negotiations to my advantage.

PSYCHO-COMMERCIAL PROFILE OF THE ORI SELLER

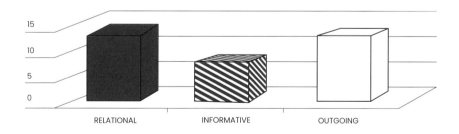

COMMERCIAL FOCUS AND DYNAMICS

In sales, you are focused on achieving your personal goals. You do this by enthusiastically convincing the customer of what you think is the best solution to his challenge. You want to make an impact and will go through hell for your customers, even if this means shaking things up a bit within your organization. You like to challenge prospects and customers, and during a challenging dialogue you show them that collaboration is an obvious choice. People appreciate the fact that you get business done and switch gears quickly to meet their needs. You have a natural talent for being strong in challenging negotiations without giving the customer the impression that this is at the expense of their added value.

PROFESSIONAL VALUES AND STANDARDS

- Powerful inquiry
- Shift quickly with customer needs in mind
- Convince customer of the best solution
- Transfer positive energy to the customer

- Honest
- Challenging
- Enforce decisions
- Work autonomously

CUSTOMER RELATIONS

Favorite customer

To-the-point customers who want to switch quickly and make decisions. Customers who do not shy away from a challenging negotiation and with whom the vendor can maintain his autonomy during the implementation of the solution.

Stretch customer

Hesitant customers who will not allow themselves to be convinced and slow down the sales process with detailed questions. Customers who show a 'hurt' response to challenging comments and questions.

PSYCHO-COMMERCIAL PROFILE OF THE OIR SALESMAN

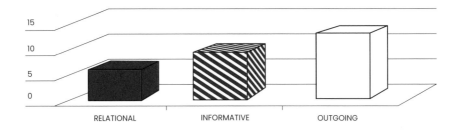

COMMERCIAL FOCUS AND DYNAMICS

In sales, the fastest and strongest wins. You convince customers with smart and decisive solutions. You have a charismatic professional image and impress during negotiations with well-founded arguments. People appreciate that you work efficiently and in a structured way. You have a natural talent for giving dynamic and clear presentations and drawing people into lines of thinking that lead to professional collaboration. You do not want to be influenced by distracting factors during the sales process and like to work in an independent manner.

PROFESSIONAL VALUES AND STANDARDS

- Effective solutions
- Hard worker
- Convince customers with results
- Powerful negotiator
- To-the-point sales story
- Clear presentations
- Enforce decisions
- Independence

CUSTOMER RELATIONS

Favorite customer	Stretch customer
Customers who know what they want and decide on the basis of well-founded arguments. Customers who do not include subjective parameters in the commercial process.	Emotional customers who base their decision on the 'click' they have with the seller. Hesitant customers who slow down the process and obstruct your goals.

THE OIR SELLER'S COMMERCIAL MOTTO:

Customers want to be convinced with powerful arguments. I achieve my commercial goal by using proven strategies and building a well-oiled sales machine.

Most common questions and concerns about self-typing

Self-observation is a process in which doubt can surface, which is good. It means that you are looking at things from a new perspective. Here you will find the most common questions and concerns about self-typing, along with their answers.

I recognize myself in all three channels of trust.
Great! That is normal and it is also the core message of this book. Every person can think, feel and take action! However, every individual has also started to 'overuse' a certain channel during his life, especially in situations that were exceptionally enjoyable or exceptionally painful. Everyone remembers the compliments he received in his youth: how strong you are (O), how smart you are (I), how sweet you are (R) and all the variations on these themes. Throughout our development we started to identify ourselves with these pats on the back and stay true to the expectation of those who cared for us.

Additionally, we went into 'hiding' at moments when life was hurtful or disappointing. Some people fled to their brains and have since become masters of 'foreseeing'. Others hid themselves in their heart region and started 'sensing'. A third group started to use the abdominal energy intensively in order to 'do'. In this way, we have given small and large injuries a place in our lives. This 'trusted' manner of dealing with stress and fear has stayed with us and we fall back on it when our system is on high alert.

Of course, choosing our channel of trust was not a conscious process, but it did create a preference for a certain RIO style. This behavioral preference is visible to many people today and presents itself in moments of distrust. So, first of all look at your natural behavior in uncomfortable situations. Are you mainly friendly, reticent or dominant in these moments?

Furthermore, it helps to look at what comes effortlessly to you. Your body and mind are so familiar with your RIO behavioral style that you perform some actions fully automatically. It is just like brushing your teeth in the bathroom each morning.
  » Relational people find it quite easy to listen to others and stand in the background. They do so as a reflex in tense situations where they want to restore calm.
  » Informative people effortlessly analyze situations and automatically notice things that are amiss. They will spontaneously place their finger on fallacies in stressful situations.
  » Outgoing people like to use their power to set things in motion. They take a strong lead in situations they distrust.

I am different in different contexts.

That is possible! RIO is a behavioral model and behavior has a context. Most people behave differently with friends than how they do at work, in a relaxed or tense atmosphere. Two questions are important here:

1 Does your behavior depend on the situation and the people around you? If so, ask yourself: What is the reason? Do you do it out of sympathy and not to offend someone? Then this points to the relational channel of trust. Or do you do it consciously so as to be seen as sympathetic, in order to then convince people and achieve your goals? Then this points to the outgoing channel of trust.

2 Do you behave differently depending on the context and your role? If so, that indicates an informative preference. Informative people attach importance to the rules of conduct and expectations that apply in a specific context and role. They see clear differences in their behavior as brother, partner, colleague, manager, participating member or chairman of the sports club.

I behave differently as a customer from how I do as a salesperson.

That is possible. It is important to home in on the aspect of trust. How do you behave as a customer and as a salesperson when trust is lacking? Are you a friendly (R), reluctant (I) or challenging (O) customer? It is good to make a distinction between important and unimportant purchases. Your RIO preference is then clearer during a large purchase.

In addition, it makes sense to look at moments when you, as a salesperson, are working with a familiar versus a new product. How do you sell a new product and what do you need to gain trust? Positive reactions from your customers (R), technical and usage information about the product (I), or visible impact of the product (O)?

I am a chameleon; I automatically adapt to the client.

Every talented salesman is adaptable. Nevertheless, of all the seller types, those with a strong outgoing channel describe themselves as chameleons most often. They match the client's behavioral style to achieve their goals. It is, however, important to note that the extent to which sales reps 'think' they are adapting is generally greater than their actual adaptations. During field coaching we have noted that the sales rep's natural behavior still shines through strongly despite alleged chameleon behavior.

I am of a different nationality, so what about cultural differences?

We have used RIO intensively over the past 10 years in international projects involving people from all five continents. It is true that each culture has specific characteristics that are important in business dealings. These have been described in detail by researcher Erin Meyer.[7] In addition to cultural traditions, there are psychological differences within each community that ensure individual diversity between people of the same origin. RIO has proven valuable in every international project in identifying behavioral differences and making them manageable within the field of sales.

I do not like being pigeonholed!

Every thorough psychological model aims to pigeonhole people. Our genetic predisposition combined with upbringing and life course have made us unique people, with specific advantages and disadvantages. Each model is a simplification of reality, just as a sketch of an object is not the object itself. Your RIO preference can be thought of as a 'photo' of the way you currently relate to other people, based on your head, heart and abdominal balance. The goal is to evolve, and RIO gives you a clear starting point to escape from the pigeonhole we are all in, that of our current thinking, feeling and acting. The next chapter of this book will help you take a step towards full maturity and integration.

RIO online self-test

If your RIO preference is not clear to you after this chapter and you would like to take a test, then you can find one via this link: www.blinc.be/nl/people-touch-customer-making.

10 TURN YOURSELF INTO A COMPREHENSIVE RIO SALESPERSON

'Become the person who would attract

the results you seek.'

— JIM CATHCART

Starting point: from the inside out

WHAT ARE WE GOING TO DO?

Are you ready to go 'the extra mile' and develop the comprehensive RIO sales-person within yourself? In previous chapters we focused RIO on the customer. You learned valuable skills with which you can better connect with others. Now it is time to place yourself in the developmental process. The focus of the following pages will not be on the client, but on yourself.

The three RIO channels are three dynamics that exist within you. No matter how well you learn to connect, you will never be able to adapt to the client 100%. And that is a good thing too! The idea is not that you erase yourself as a person, it is above all the intention to be your complete self (and that is not who you think you are and is definitely much more than your RIO type).

In this chapter we will take the step together to balance the three dynamics within you. When you integrate RIO, you demonstrate authentic behavior that is automatically tailored to the client and the situation. You no longer have to make an effort to 'imitate' the client's RIO preference; the connection arises spontaneously because you allow the dynamics to flow from within.

Imagine that you no longer have to stretch to another channel of trust, but that all your channels are already integrated. What would that mean for your way of selling and your results? What could that mean for every potential customer?

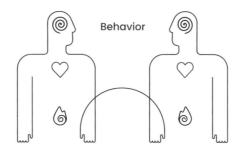

Behavior

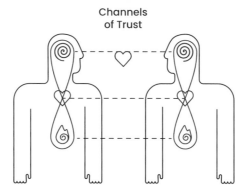

Channels
of Trust

WHY WOULD YOU WANT TO DO THAT?

There are several reasons for developing yourself into a comprehensive
RIO salesperson.

» The world is in full transformation. The sales profession must follow.
Evolution does not consist of doing 'more of the same' – read: learning
even stronger competencies, using even smarter techniques, etc. No,
the next step is inner growth, freeing yourself from the automatic RIO
patterns that you have developed over time.

» Furthermore, conscious adaptation costs energy. It is a process in
which you have to think about your choice of words, intonation,
the larger sales process, your body language, dynamics and so on. It
mainly costs energy with customers who prefer your underdeveloped
channel. When you balance the three RIO dynamics within yourself,
you automatically connect with the client on a deeper level. This creates a flow between the two of you through which the client is inspired
by your way of being.

» You are more than your RIO type! When people come into contact with RIO, they acquire a language to name what they actually already know. They can name their most dominant dynamics. However, when they identify with this self-typing, RIO ceases to be a means of evolution, and instead traps them in their behavior! Perhaps you will recognize yourself in one of the following thoughts:

'I'm an "R" so I'm a huge team player, I prefer not to be involved in complicated strategic discussions and, while we're at it, be a bit nice to me, because I can't stand unfriendly people.'

'I'm an "O", I sometimes blurt out something that's rude but, yeah, that's just how I am.'

'I'm an "I", I really can't bear it when people just show up to a meeting unprepared. Is that so hard to do?!'

Deep down, you of course know that you are not an R, I or O. You are much more than any single one of them and are first and foremost your *Self*.

HOW DOES RIO INTEGRATION WORK?

ASSESS

You cannot change what you are unaware of. Only insight can bring movement. If you wish to become a comprehensive salesperson, knowing your RIO preference is the first step. But it goes much further than that. In this chapter we will teach you to look at the reasons why your RIO preference first arose and what protective function it had. It is important for every RIO type to see, recognize, and honor his underlying fears.

'If you change the way you look at things,

the things you look at change.'

– WAYNE DYER

HONOR

Honoring what is already there is the basis for inner growth. When you try to break a pattern by pushing it away or ignoring it, it only becomes more ingrained. Remember that your mechanisms originated from a protective reflex, something that was extremely valuable and necessary in your life. They have taken you to where you are now. Honoring is, therefore, acknowledging the positive intentions behind your automatic patterns. This is the only way to create space and trust to allow for a shift in your inner dynamics.

EXPERIENCE

A third important principle for achieving RIO integration is experience. You can only achieve integration when you have the courage to open up and practice. Without experience your system will not open up, and why should it? It is like learning to swim theoretically and then jumping into the deep end. You would not do that either. The logical progression is from water habituation to technique training. Working with your inner system is like learning to swim, it takes more than theory.

THE FOLLOWING TERMS MAY FRIGHTEN YOU FOR A MOMENT

THE SELF – THE EGO

You may have noticed that we have mentioned your *Self* a few times now. What are we speaking about? We are speaking about the Self with a capital S, your true Self, and not the little ego-self. Your ego is that part of you that fully identifies with your outer form, your mind, your emotions and role (e.g. 'I'm a sales manager'). The Self is the consciousness that encompasses all these possibilities. You are not the R, the I or the O of our model. They are just strategies you have learned over time. You can say that your Self represents your full potential in which you have fully integrated all the RIO components. At that point you no longer have preferences for one particular dynamic, you are all three at once and in a balanced state.

'The Ego is born out of the need for self-protection.

The Self is the intelligence that inspires it.'

– FROM UPANISHADS – *THE VEDAS*

CONSCIOUS EGO

The conscious ego is a term from *voice dialogue*, a method through which you can explore the different dynamics within yourself.[8] Building a conscious ego is a dynamic process in which you are able to experience both your primary personality components as well as those you rejected. Without the conscious ego you would permanently be on autopilot, and the conscious ego gives insight into your automatic habits, but also brings you in touch with what is underneath. By understanding and honoring what is already there, there is freedom to choose. Do you step into the automatic pattern or can you allow the other dynamics within yourself to speak?

ENERGY

Not really a word to be scared of! After all, everything consists of energy, nothing new there. That is true, the only thing that will take some getting used to is the fact that we are challenging you to work with the energy from all three centers (head – heart – abdomen). Balancing these centers is an inner contact sport. You have to experience it, otherwise it remains abstract. You can philosophize about it, without actually changing. Feeling, seeing, hearing, smelling and tasting the energy with your inner senses is what creates the movement and that is what we are going to do.

INNER GROWTH

When some people hear 'inner growth' what comes to mind is: 'Why should I grow, am I not good enough already?' This reaction says a great deal about how people think about inner work. Too often people think that there must be something wrong with them before starting self-development. However, it only means freeing yourself from the restrictive patterns that influence each of us.

Inner growth is mainly about awareness. Only that which you are aware of can be set in motion; only then can you do something about it. The result is that you somehow become richer. You are more flexible in your thinking, you are less annoyed, you can see and appreciate more perspectives at once. You also know your own fears and struggles, but instead of suppressing them through all kinds of mechanisms (your patterns), you start recognizing and acknowledging them and working with them. You are increasingly able to reach your essence, in order to use your full potential. You are able to embrace the R, the I and the O within yourself instead of feeling aversion to one or more of the dynamics.

SHADOW

By shadow, we mean the behaviors and character traits that you firmly believe you do not possess or that you do not do. The best way to recognize shadows is to look at what annoys you about other people. If you have a primary R-dynamic, then you may be immensely annoyed by dominant nothing-ventured-nothing-gained people. The O-dynamic is something you do not allow yourself, that has been pushed to the back and become a shadow component. Gradually bringing this piece back into your life creates an enormously positive impact on your interactions, both private and professional.

UNDERLYING FEARS AND THE SHADOW DYNAMICS AMONG THE RIO TYPES

Something special happens when you start to learn to work with RIO. At first old patterns strengthen themselves. That is because these behaviors are familiar and provide safety in situations where an attempt is made to do things differently. Letting go of protective structures is quite exciting. Let's now take a closer look at the fears and shadows of each RIO type.

R

The biggest fear of someone with a primarily relational channel is being left alone. By building relationships, relational people ensure that there is always someone around to connect with. Taking a closer look at this 'urge to connect' brings tension with it. For a relational person it is a big step to gain insight into this. Moreover, it is vitally important to continue to honor this primary strategy.

The shadow dynamics for an R:
- » The direct approach of the O-type; calling things for what they are is frightening to an R as it seems to compromise the relationship.
- » The aloof attitude of the I-type; to the R's mind, it seems impossible to build a relationship based on fact and reason.

I

The greatest fear of someone with a primarily informative channel is not being able to control what is going on. Losing control is to be avoided at all times. Uncertainty is unbearable. Continuing to learn, coming up with strategies and theories makes everything comprehensible and that creates peace. The need for certainty clearly means that letting go will be very frightening. Therefore, continuing to validate the intellect is crucial.

The shadow dynamics of an I:
- » Spontaneity in the interaction, being unprepared to respond to what is coming up; things relational people are good at.
- » The forcefulness of the O-dynamic; that comes across as intrusive to informative people. Things go too quickly; informative people would like time to process and understand.

O

The greatest fear of someone with a primarily outgoing channel is losing his or her autonomy. The idea of being dependent on someone else is unbearable.

Outgoing people carry a deep conviction that they have to do it alone and they are very wary of backstabbers. They have built a sturdy armor that ensures invulnerability. Behind this, however, hides an extremely sensitive heart. It is logical that its protection must be extra strong.

The shadow dynamics of the O:
» The sensitivity of R-types; feeling all the emotions, not only anger.
» The slow decision making of I-types; in other words, being with your-self in peace and quiet.

'To confront a man with his shadow

is to show him his own light.'

– C.G. JUNG

In addition to the shadow side, everyone is also uncertain about how the people around them will react in the event of change. What will they do if that kind and sweet colleague suddenly stops saying 'yes' to every request? Is there room for a second loudmouth on the team? What will the reaction be if the tough manager suddenly becomes vulnerable?

Working with RIO does not leave you unchanged. It is perfectly normal that after being introduced to RIO you react more pronouncedly R, I or O than before. That is a clever strategy by your ego to keep everything the way it is. It is also never the intention to 'unlearn' or 'get rid of' anything. Every RIO dynamic is valuable and has brought you to where you are today.

In order to evolve, it is important to, first of all, learn compensatory skills, then it is worthwhile to go beyond the level of competence.

During RIO integration you make the journey within yourself, and your trans-formations have an impact on all the systems in which you live:
» your customer relationships;
» your team;
» your organization;
» your family;
» ...

Are you ready to become acquainted with the complete version of your Self?

The logical levels as a guide

——

**BECOMING AN INTEGRATED SELLER
WITH THE LOGICAL LEVELS AS A DIRECTION INDICATOR**

In the early 1990s Robert Dilts introduced the hierarchy of logical levels, based on Gregory Bateson's work *Steps to an Ecology of Mind*.

The logical levels provide an analytical model that offers insight into the way people communicate, function and change. It shows a hierarchy within the factors that determine human behavior, with each higher level having a direct influence on the levels below it.

The lower levels are more concrete and tangible, the higher levels are more complex and abstract.

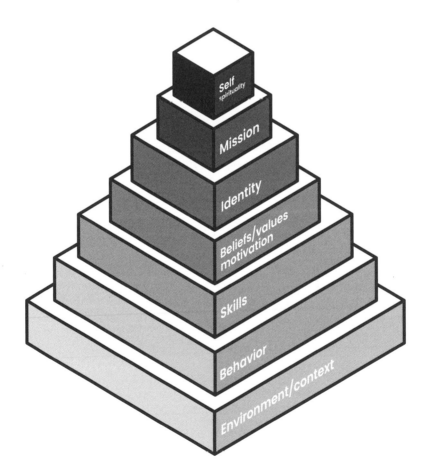

The way the logical levels operate can be described as follows:

» Each higher level directly impacts the levels underneath it.
» Change at a lower level can bring about change at a higher level.
» Change at a higher level will bring about change at all lower levels.
» The solution to a problem is never at the level where the problem arises, but higher.

AN EXAMPLE

Suppose a vendor is having difficulty applying the RIO sales skills. He keeps struggling to adapt his behavior to the potential client. In other circumstances, however, he learns new skills easily and it is striking that this is precisely what he is now failing to do. You might conclude that the problem is situated at the skill level (he cannot manage it). However, continuing to practice these competences will bring little progress. It is then interesting to go one level higher and look for the key at the level of belief.

Suppose the salesperson in our example has an OIR dynamic and he is convinced that the challenging approach always works best: 'Sales is a martial art where the strongest wins.' He sees no added value in the RIO story. To get this salesperson to work with the RIO methodology, change is needed at the level of beliefs (martial arts) and possibly at the level of his identity (I am a winner!). When the salesperson is guided on the level of belief, his behavior will automatically evolve. In this way, he will be able to apply the RIO skills to every potential client from then on.

When skills, beliefs and behavior within a certain context are congruent with each other, as well as with the higher identity, mission and Self, we have what is called 'alignment'. All levels are working together and reinforcing each other.

THE LEVELS IN BRIEF

ENVIRONMENT/CONTEXT

The environment or context are the time- and location-specific circumstances in which people act. It is what we react to, what surrounds us. This could be other people, the family, the circle of friends, the customers, etc. In short, everything outside the individual. It is an answer to the questions: who, what, where, when and in what role?

BEHAVIOR

Behavior is what you do, your attitude, gestures, your comings and goings, your voice, etc. Your behavior consists of specific actions within a context. You can consciously steer your behavior, but unconsciously the higher levels actually exert a greater impact on behavior. It is an answer to the questions: What are you doing? What is observable?

SKILLS/COMPETENCES

Skills are the abilities, qualities, talents, insights, strategies and tactics you have at your disposal. They give direction to your behavior through a plan. They are the answers to the questions: What can you do? How do you tackle something? What are your resources? What do you still have to learn?

BELIEFS/VALUES/MOTIVATION

Beliefs are claims about yourself, your company, others, the world around you, that are true for you. They are not facts but personal generalizations, criteria, standards, values and expectations. It is the level at which motivation arises. Beliefs and values give direction to your behavior. They are the answers to the questions: What do you believe? What is important to you? What is beyond dispute? Why do you do what you do?

IDENTITY

Your identity is how you think about yourself as a person; your self-image and self-esteem are linked to this. It is the answer to the question: Who or what are you?

MISSION

This is your life's mission. It consists of intuitions about the greater whole and your vocation within it. It is the foundation of your existence and the answer to the questions: Why are you here? What is the meaning of your presence? Where are you coming from? What do you bring?

SPIRITUALITY/SELF

Spirituality is part of a whole that transcends our individuality. People belong to a family, a community and a global system. In the same way, our personality belongs to our soul – a soul that is much broader than the individual we think we are. It is the answer to the question: Who or what transcends me?

RIO AT THE COMPETENCE LEVEL: COMPLEMENTARY SKILLS

Up until this point, the RIO methodology has been described at the level of skill. You have been given knowledge and tips that will help you:

- » assess your client's channel of trust;
- » adapt your behavior to the customer at any stage of the process, even if it is a stretch for you.

As a closing word on RIO at the level of skill, we will now describe the complementary skills that produce a massive shift for each of the RIO vendor types. Feel free to call this the 'fast repair kit' for any type of vendor. Be warned! You will not be keen to learn these skills, but they will have a huge impact on your results!

THE R-TOOLKIT FOR SALESPEOPLE WHOSE RELATIONAL CHANNEL OF TRUST COMES LAST (OIR, IOR)

Preparation

- » Write out the mission and higher purpose of your organization. What difference do you want to make in the world?
- » Check Glassdoor.com to get an idea of the prospect's organizational culture.
- » Check traicie.com to gauge your customer's RIO type in advance.
- » Yoga, mindfulness, connecting communication.

Opening

- » Connect with your customers via RIO.

Capture

- » SPIN selling.
- » Ask open-ended, in-depth questions.
- » Listen actively.
- » Paraphrase: Do I correctly understand that...?
- » Learn to ask after and sense VENCAP purchase motives.

Presentation

- » Learn to present without supporting material (PowerPoint, Showpad).
- » Speak in terms of personal customer benefits.
- » Maintain connection during the presentation.

Feedback

» Let the customer speak.
» Elaborate on emotional customer feedback.
» Paraphrase: Do I correctly understand that...?

Co-creation

» Co-create a tailored solution.

Engagement

» Have patience.

Implementation

» Handle complaints with a customer-focus.

Via the download page (https://www.blinc.be/nl/mensen-raken-klanten-maken) you will find literature and tutorials to learn these competences in concrete terms!

THE I-TOOLKIT FOR SALESPEOPLE WHOSE INFORMATIVE CHANNEL OF TRUST COMES LAST (ORI, ROI)

Preparation

» Spot business trends.
» Prepare market analysis and segmentation.
» Build a go-to-market strategy.
» Learn Google search tricks to find information on prospects.
» Learn to play chess.
» Rhetoric, logic and syllogisms.

Opening

» Present the company's history.

Capture

» Use the Miller Heiman Group's blue, green and gold sheets.
» Use the SCOTSMAN's structured questioning to map out the decision-making process.

Presentation

» Make use of professional presentation tools (PowerPoint, Showpad, product sheet).
» Provide an objective list of the product's pros and cons.
» Present case studies.

Feedback
» Expand on the feedback objectively.
» Answer critical questions.
» Influence the customer's frame of mind.

Co-creation
» Use design thinking.

Engagement
» Make a risk analysis.
» Create a clear customer file.
» Employ strategic closing techniques.

Implementation
» Draw up and follow a project plan.

Via the download page (https://www.blinc.be/nl/mensen-raken-klanten-maken) you will find literature and tutorials to learn these competences in concrete terms!

THE O-TOOLKIT FOR SALESPEOPLE WHOSE OUTGOING CHANNEL OF TRUST COMES LAST (RIO, IRO))

Preparation
» Format an ICP (ideal customer profile, which can be sold quickly).
» Prepare an operational plan to approach the territory.
» Establish KPIs, targets and dashboards.
» Check business analysis websites (Trendstop, Graydon, Creditsafe, NBB, Companyweb) to screen prospective business results.
» Do strength training (bodybuilding, martial arts).

Opening
» Get your customer excited.
» Deliver pitches.

Capture
» Ask confronting questions.

Presentation
» Use outgoing body language.
» Use powerful language (eliminate ambiguous expressions).
» Visibly convey enthusiasm.

Feedback
» Learn to block feedback.
» Repeat the benefit of your point of view.

Co-creation
» Think in a solution-focused manner.

Engagement
» Calculate the return on investment and defend the price.
» Challenge the status quo and share the practical 'next steps'.
» Develop negotiation, persuasion and closing techniques.
» Be quick to respond during follow-up.

Implementation
» Getting things done!

Via the download page (https://www.blinc.be/nl/mensen-raken-klanten-maken) you will find literature and tutorials to learn these competences in concrete terms!

___

NEXT LEVEL RIO

Now that you know what to do on a skill level, you are ready for the next step. In chapter 4 we referred to the neuroscience behind the different centers of intelligence in the body and their neural networks. What is of note here is the knowledge that the three channels of trust are present within each of us. Everyone has a head brain, a heart brain and an abdominal brain; there is no doubt about that. The next step is to use the RIO model to gain insight into which of the three centers you use most. In other words, which dynamic have you used most successfully over time and which have you neglected, resulting in certain qualities taking a back seat? The sales profession helps you to clarify this question.

When you come into contact with customers, different experiences are possible:
1   The interaction is good and both parties understand each other immediately.
2   The interaction is neutral, not bad but not particularly good either.
3   You feel annoyed and notice that you and your client are on different wavelengths.

From a RIO perspective, the following occurs: when the interaction is good, you have both hooked into a common channel of trust. An exchange is taking place in which you are engaging your favorite dynamic. Internally, you are connected to your dominant energy.

In the case of annoyance, you are most likely faced with a customer with a different RIO dynamic. This generates resistance and 'drains' energy. You are resisting the customer's dynamic but at the same time also your own buried channel of trust. At that moment, you are not only out of touch with the client but, more importantly, out of touch with your Self. Your customer is inviting you to personal growth!

The wonderful thing about sales is that salespeople do not have to look beyond the work environment when it comes to self-development training. Every interaction with customers is an opportunity for inner growth. How great is that?

WHICH LOGICAL LEVELS ARE WE ENTERING NOW?

In order to achieve personal growth, we must explore the levels of beliefs, identity, mission and Self. You are now entering an inner movement, discovering, strengthening and integrating the other channels of trust within yourself so as to enter your natural state of being.

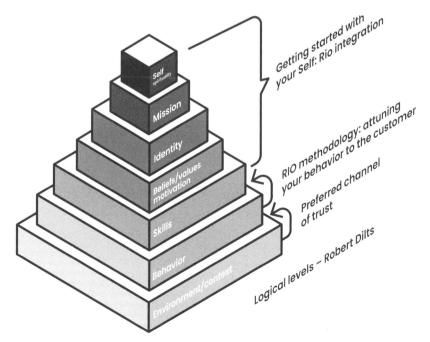

Integration occurs when you transcend the personality level and make contact with that which is broader than ourself. We plug in at the level of spirituality to connect with our full potential. We gain insight into our life's mission and acquire a more expansive picture of who we are; this situates our beliefs and behaviors within a broader reality.

How you work at these higher levels will become clear in the exercises that follow. Stay tuned!

Warm-up exercises

We will start this inner journey with a few exercises in which you will get to know your three dynamics and become proficient at inner perception. The latter requires practice, especially to learn to interpret and take seriously what you notice.

Then, we will go through the logical levels one by one, supplementing each level with one or more exercises. The end goal is that you are not only able to communicate with your three dynamics, but also that you align them with each other and with your Self.

BALANCE IN EACH CENTER

Let's take a look at each channel of trust. Focus your attention on yourself and do not be preoccupied with assessing clients or colleagues.

We know that our three dynamics are fundamentally different because they work with their own goals, their own language and their own criteria. Your heart, your head and your belly each approach the world in their specific way.

Your abdominal dynamic is focused on:
- » self-protection;
- » core identity;
- » mobilization, action, movement.

Your heart dynamic is focused on:
- » connection and affection;
- » feeling;
- » values and criteria.

Your head dynamic is focused on:
> » thinking;
> » giving meaning;
> » cognitive perception.

Each of the centers communicates and acts differently, focusing on their own interests and on the area in which they are experts.

Every dynamic can be in balance, in overdrive or in underdrive. A state of balance does not mean inactivity, but instead a nice alternation between activity and rest. If you compare it to a driving a car, balance is accelerating (action) and braking (rest) at the appropriate moments. Driving without jerking. When you are balanced in your three centers, you react optimally to the world and experience joy, clarity and energy.

A channel of trust in overdrive means that there is only gas and no rest. In this state one or more dynamics react from a danger response: fight or flight!

A state of underdrive causes you to over-brake, which eventually leads you to stop. That is literally what happens when your dynamics are in continuous underdrive. There is a 'freeze state' in which despair and depression arise. You can stop reading for a moment and imagine a number of sales situations. Picture yourself in one of those situations and examine with an open, non-judgmental mind whether your primary RIO channel was in balance or overdrive. And what happened to your least favorite center? It is possible that it was in underdrive by default.

The following table is an aid in determining your inner state.[9]

ABDOMINAL CENTER

Underdrive	Balance	Overdrive
Uncertain / unsafe	Healthy self-preservation	Stressed out
Depression	Relaxed / calm	Overanxious
Self-protection	Well-being	Self-harm
Fear: freezing / retreating	Courage	Fear: fight / flight
Anesthesia / hibernation	Action / gut motivation / drive	Impulsiveness
Hunger	Hunger / satiation	Disgust

HEART CENTER

Underdrive	Balance	Overdrive
Emotionally subdued	Peace / forgiveness	Anger
Hopeless	Hope	Desperation
Sadness / unhappiness	Joy	Mania / hysteria
Blind trust	Trust	Distrust
Loneliness	Connection	Wariness
Emotionally unfazed	Appreciation / gratitude	Obligation
Apathy / uncaring	Compassion	Vindictiveness
Indifference	Love	Hatred
Focused on oneself	Generosity	Greed / avarice
Emotionally unconnected	Equality Emotional security	Jealousy / aggression Emotional uncertainty
Emotionally blind	Emotional truth and wisdom	Fickleness / lying / emotional deception
Aimlessness	Passion (dreams / goals / values)	Obsession

HEAD CENTER

Underdrive	Balance	Overdrive
Caught in the details	In the present	Out of time
Dissociation	Meta-awareness	Subjective reality
Single reality	Balanced perspective / integrated view	Several simultaneous realities
Going in mental / subjective circles	Flow state	Mental leaps
Convergent thinking	Creativity	Divergent thinking
Fixation	Curiosity	Distraction
Logically structured learning	Transformational / generative learning	Survival / streetwise learning

Repeat this inner scan for different situations and take a notebook to record the differences. The more open you are, the greater the insights.

» Good, smooth interactions
» Bumpier interactions
» Annoying, bad interactions

PERCEIVE WITH YOUR INNER SENSES

When we talk about each dynamic's own language, we mean it literally. Each center provides you with information in its own way. The language of the head dynamic can be recognized through internal words, images and sounds. The languages of the heart and abdominal dynamic are in some ways similar and communicate through physical sensations, symbolic language, dreams and visions. In addition, the heart dynamic uses emotions to make things clear.

When you feel nausea during a certain conversation, your abdominal dynamic is sending you the signal that something is amiss. Sensations are often more subtle and require an alertness to pick them up.

In the following exercises, we invite you to sharpen your inner senses and allow the answers to emerge from your different centers. There will certainly be a tendency to play it safe and to approach these exercises with just your 'head dynamic'. Know that you will then only receive limited information.

Valuable information can take unexpected forms. An example will make this clear. When, after questioning one of your channels, you see the image of a duck, you may not like it at first. Resist the tendency to regard this information as ridiculous and do not ignore the image. What presents itself is fundamentally important, the only thing missing is an understanding of the image.

To clarify the information, you must work through free associations. The questions to ask yourself are:
   » What does a duck mean to me?
   » What energy is involved?
   » What do I associate with a duck?

It is these associations that you can move forward with. When you discover that you associate a duck with softness, that is the answer to the initial question. For the sake of clarity, we would like to mention that you have the following inner senses: inner seeing, hearing, smell, feel and taste. Besides images, you can also expect physical sensations and sounds and, to a lesser extent, inner smells and tastes.

SHORT EXERCISE TO EXPLORE THE THREE CENTERS

Sit down, relax. You can do this exercise while reading. It is important that you read slowly, feel and perceive clearly, and take enough time to pause between the different parts. Set all distractions aside.

Start breathing in and out quietly and become aware of the rhythm of your breathing, pay close attention to your inhalation.

» How deeply do you breathe?
» Can you feel your breath flowing in? How does that feel?

When you are totally focused on your breathing, what happens to your thoughts? Do they jump in all directions? Or do they calm down? Do you go along with your thoughts or can you stay in charge and stay with your breathing? We invite you, when your attention slips, to gently bring it back each time.

Just keep breathing deliberately for a minute or two.

Place a hand on your belly. Pay full attention to your belly, as if there is nothing but your belly. Allow an image of a fire or a shining ball of energy to appear there. What does it look like? Does it have a color? How big is it? What else do you notice? See and feel, without judgment, just observe.

Then shift your focus to your heart center. Put a hand on your heart and give this area your full attention. Create an image of a fire or an energy sphere here as well. What does it look like? Does it have a color? How big is it? What else do you notice? See and feel, without judgment, just observe.

Now do the same with your head. Place a hand on your head and give this area your full attention. Allow a new image of a fire or an energy sphere to emerge there. What does it look like? Does it have a color? How big is it? What else do you notice? Again, see and feel without judgment, just observe.

In your mind, now feel and see the three centers at the same time. Which sphere (or fire) strikes you the most? Is there one you cannot perceive as well as the others? Which one is the largest?

Then finish this exercise and note down your experience in writing. What do you get out of this exercise?

For starters, you have made contact with every channel of trust. If you did things right, you did not approach the abdominal and heart dynamics from your head, but instead made direct contact through your attention. In this exercise even your head dynamic was brought to your attention in a way that is different from daily rational thinking. Do you have any idea which energy is easiest for you to summon and which is the hardest?

___

BELIEFS – VALUES – MOTIVATION

Now that we have made contact with the three centers, it is time to review the logical levels. The first level above skills is that of beliefs. A belief is something you know, a firm opinion. For example, you are convinced that the products you sell are the best on the market. This belief will have a different impact on your behavior than the belief that your products are mediocre.

Beliefs influence your behavior in an unconscious way. They motivate or demotivate you and shape what you do. It is important to keep in mind that beliefs are not reality, but shape what you consider to be reality. Feel free to read that last sentence again! Your beliefs are not reality; they are just a part of reality. All other beliefs are also true for the people who hold them.

Beliefs have a direct impact on your behavior, your feelings and your environment.

Two examples:
1   The effect of placebo medication can be attributed to the belief that you have taken a drug that works well. If you have any doubts about the medicine, the effect will be diminished or non-existent.
2   In a study on the impact of beliefs, students were divided into two groups, high and low IQs, after testing their IQ. The group with high scores was told by the teacher that they were less gifted and the group with low scores that they were talented. At the end of the school year, students were tested again. The test scores were significantly different. The less gifted pupils had become 'smarter' and the brighter pupils had regressed. The only determining factor for this evolution was the initial belief planted by the teacher.

Both examples underline the power of beliefs. It is the impact of the self-fulfilling prophecy or, to put it in other words, what you believe becomes reality.

EMERGENCE OF BELIEFS

The most important beliefs arise when we are young as a result of our upbringing, contact with impactful people, the culture we live in and the successes and failures we have experienced. These early imprints can be persistent. Suppose you have the rock-solid conviction that you are not a strong 'closer'. This is confirmed time and time again by last-minute deals. This conviction will not change simply by telling yourself that you can sell well. The reason for this is that your entire system refuses to believe what you say. You have to do deeper work to get things moving. Under the 'I'm not a closer' belief there may be an even more fundamental belief that has to do with values. Your family may have originally looked down on salespeople. Maybe phrases like 'all salespeople are cheaters' were uttered. This creates a link between an adopted belief and the value of honesty. If you were a good salesperson, you would no longer uphold the value of honesty. In a crazy way you stay true to your value of honesty by not selling well.

Our convictions are not only pictures of the past, they are also the blueprints of our future actions.

WHAT DO BELIEFS SOUND LIKE?

Sentences with:

If... then...
I can't...
I could...
I should've...
I shouldn't...
I know that...

Positive beliefs are supportive and negative beliefs are limiting. Fortunately, beliefs are flexible and can be reversed. It is time to explore the beliefs linked to your RIO profile.

- **Preparation**

Sit quietly and focus on your breathing. Follow the movement of the airflow and pay particular attention to it. The intention is that you turn your attention within and leave fleeting thoughts for what they are. Focusing on your breathing is always a good starting point. You will come across this in further exercises.

While following your breathing with curiosity and an open mind, turn your attention to your preferred channel of trust. Starting from R, focus your attention to your heart. Starting from I, focus your attention on your head. If you are starting from O, focus your attention on your belly.

The order in which you conduct this interview is the same as your RIO profile.

Put three chairs in the room, one for your heart (R), one for your head (I) and one for your abdominal intelligence (O).

When you place the chairs, the intention is that you do this with intense focus. In other words, you are only doing this exercise and placing the chairs. Go to each chair again and reconfirm what each chair stands for (head – heart – abdomen).

Sit on the chair that represents your first RIO channel. Now allow yourself to become that center of intelligence and speak from that center.

Ask your primary center the following questions:
Note: do not expect a verbatim answer but be alert to images, physical sensations, colors, sounds, etc.: symbolic language.

» How are you doing here?
» How do you express yourself in <*your name*>'s daily life?
» What exactly do you do?
» How do you do that?
» What is important to you?
» What are you willing to invest time, money and energy into?
» When did you take over in <*your name*>'s life for the first time? What was going on at that time?
» What do you bring <*your name*>?
» What would happen to <*your name*> if you were less present?
» Is there anything else you would like to say to <*your name*>?

When you are done interviewing your primary center, stand up quietly. Write down some key words but do not try to analyze or explain anything yet. Stay in that state of inner focus and then go to the next chair, the second center of your RIO profile.

Ask your second center the following questions:
- » How are you doing here?
- » At what times may you be present within <*your name*>?
- » How do you express yourself in <*your name*>'s daily life?
- » What exactly do you do?
- » How do you do that?
- » What is important to you?
- » What are you willing to invest time, money and energy into?
- » What can you bring <*your name*>? And can you do that frequently?
- » What would happen to <*your name*> if you were more present?
- » Is there anything else you would like to say to <*your name*>?

When you have finished the interview with your second center, stand up quietly. Write down some key words, but still do not analyze or explain anything. Stay in that state of inner focus and then go to the next chair, the center of your least present RIO dynamic.

Ask your third center the following questions:
- » How are you doing here?
- » Are there moments when you may be present in <*your name*>?
- » How would you express yourself in <*your name*>'s daily life if you could do so more frequently?
- » Tell me, how would you do that?
- » What is important to you?
- » If it were up to you, what would you invest time, money and energy into?
- » If you could be more present within <*your name*>, what could that mean for him/her?
- » Is there anything else you would like to say to <*your name*>?

When you have finished the interview with your third RIO channel, stand up quietly and write down some key words underneath.

Sit again on the chair where you first started this exercise. A neutral chair, where you are your entire Self and not just one of the centers. Take a moment to feel; what do you feel?

» Interview with your heart dynamic (R)
» Interview with your head dynamic (I)
» Interview with your abdominal dynamic (O)

Have a look at what you noted as your total Self. What do you notice? Which beliefs stand out?

Are there any differences between the centers?

IN CONTACT WITH OTHERS
Now that you have explored the beliefs linked to your channels of trust, it is time to discover what happens when you come into contact with opposing RIO dynamics.

For the next exercise, remember a concrete situation with a client – one in which the client had a different RIO dynamic from you. Take a situation where the interaction went poorly; this is where you can get the most information.

- **Position 1 = Myself**

Imagine that situation happening now. Notice again where you are, what the customer looks like, hear yourself and the customer speak. Look through your own eyes at the customer and the situation.

Then check each of the following things with yourself:

» What do I see around me?
» How do I look at the other person, what do I see the other person doing?
» What do I do?
» What do I say?
» What thoughts do I have:
  - about the client?
  - about myself?
  - about the situation?
» What do I feel inside?
» Are there any emotions?
» Do I have physical sensations?
» What do I do or what would I prefer to do?

»   How do I react to the other?
»   What state are my three centers in?
   • Overdrive?
   • Balance?
   • Underdrive?

To do this, use the 'overdrive'-'underdrive' tables from a few pages back and circle the words that match the state of each center.

Do you notice anything? What center takes the upper hand here? Which one of the three retreats?

   • **Position 2 = The other**
In the same situation, now change positions. Examine the whole thing from the customer's point of view. To do that, literally move to the place that your client occupied opposite you in the conversation. Sit in his chair, so to speak. From this position go over the following questions:
   » What are your thoughts right now?
      • about the seller?
      • about yourself as a customer?
      • about the situation?
   » What do you feel in this position?
   » Are there any emotions?
   » Do you have any physical sensations?
   » What do you do or what would you prefer to do?
   » Then find out what state the three centers are in:
      • Overdrive?
      • Balance?
      • Underdrive?

Again, to do this, use the tables and circle the words that match the condition of each center, in a different color from before.

Now, when you look at the three centers from both positions, what do you notice? What information did you get from the client's point of view? Are there things you had not examined before? If it is all right, then it is just that. Through this exercise, you see the same situation from a different perspective. Literally from the customer's perspective. As mentioned before, reality in itself does not exist, but you perceive it through your perceptual filters. When you place yourself in another's shoes and feel that very fully and seriously, you get information from a different perspective, which broadens your view of reality.

- **Position 3 = Observer**

Shall we broaden the perspective a bit? Move to a position where you have an overview of the entire situation. From here you can see both yourself and your client as well as the dynamic between the two of you. Take the position of a neutral observer, as if you had nothing to do with the conversation. You are a spectator.

Watch the scene in front of you, like you are watching a film.

» What do you see happening with each of them?
» Do both parties really understand each other?
» What intention do you see in one and what intention do you see in the other?
» What does one want to achieve and what does the other want to achieve?
» How could they come to a solution together?
» In this situation, what advice would you give to the person in the first position?
» How could this advice be applied in practice? (be as specific as possible)

Note: Make sure you do not formulate advice for the client because that is unhelpful to you. The only thing you can change is yourself. Fully take that responsibility and do not place it outside yourself. The world is full of people who can explain how someone else should do things…

- **Position 1, enlarged**

Now go back to the first position, your own in the situation. Now that you have much more information about yourself, about the other person and about the dynamics between the two of you, how do things feel in this situation? Has something changed?

You can do this exercise whenever you want more insight into yourself and the other person. This method provides three perspectives from which a person can perceive an interaction between himself and others. By looking at the situation from different positions, listening and experiencing, you discover things of which you were previously unaware.

IDENTITY – MISSION – SELF

'Know thyself' read the inscription above the Oracle of Delphi. Achieving wisdom, intuition and success is a necessity, as the ancient Greeks knew. Now make it less evident. What is your first answer to the question: Who are you? The chances are that you will answer with your name, accompanied or not by your function on the work floor. 'I'm Pete, salesperson at...' But is that you? Is that your whole Self? We certainly do not think so; you are much more than that.

When we look back at the logical levels, you can see that the identity level is located above the belief level. Knowing that every change at a higher level has an impact on all of the underlying levels, it is then interesting to look deeper into your identity. Who are you?

Depending on the angle from which you approach this question, elements will be cited that are characteristic of your personality (happy, social, helpful, etc.), the social roles you fulfill (profession, being a parent, member of an association, etc.), the country and culture to which you belong, your religion and perhaps even your online identity.

No matter how many elements you mention, this list remains limiting. We are still speaking at the level of identity-building through interactions with something or someone *outside of* the Self. In psychology, however, identity is viewed as something that is established *within* the person.

We like the even broader approach taken in psychoenergetics.[10] Here, identity is viewed as a superposition within quantum physics. According to quantum mechanics, an object can inhabit all its possible states at the same time – a superposition – until it is observed. Observing an object freezes its state as a single possibility. The cat in Schrödinger's thought experiment is both alive and dead at the same time until someone actually looks inside the box.[11] Linking this to our identity, we can say that who we are at the deepest level is a 'superposition' of all our potential states at the same time. We are our full potential, a combination of all possible character traits. It is only when we interact with others or observe ourselves that one particular state reveals itself. Departing from the superposition brings us into contact with our full potential, our true Self.

The following exercise is a breathing exercise in which we will connect the three dynamics. From this aligned state within the personality, we renew the connection with the Self, making transformation possible.

First read all of the text before doing the exercise. Alternatively, you can listen to the podcast for this exercise so that we can guide you through it. Go to the website for more information: https://www.blinc.be/nl/mensen-raken-klant-en-maken.

- **The Exercise**

Sit down quietly and close your eyes. Assume a comfortable position with two feet on the ground and a straight spine. Then focus your attention on your breathing and follow the rhythmic movement of your inhalation and exhalation.

Gradually make the inhalation last as long as the exhalation. Slowly build up the duration until both movements last six beats each. If six beats is not feasible, bring it to four or five. The most important thing now is that the movements are equally as long.

Then turn your attention to the transition between the two movements. By nature, we always pause between breathing in and breathing out, but leave that aside. Make sure that there is a continuous movement, that there is neither acceleration nor deceleration. Make your breathing one flowing, even wave-like motion. That is connected breathing.

As you continue to breathe that way, turn your attention inward and visualize the wave motion of your breathing as it moves between your belly, your heart and your head. A stream running up and down the middle of your body, connecting the three centers.

Stay focused on your breathing and the inner sensations that this brings with it. Do this continuously for two minutes before continuing the exercise.

Then very consciously connect your abdominal center with your heart. You could imagine an infinity symbol, or figure eight, connecting both centers in a continuous loop. As you visualize this, continue to breathe in a connected way.

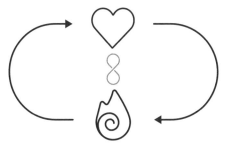

Then connect your heart and your head with another figure eight.

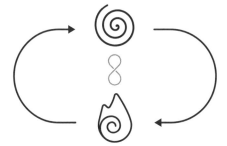

Then connect each of the three centers by situating the figure eight's center at your heart.

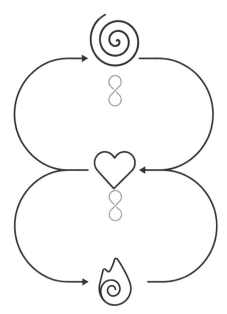

Feel this connection throughout your body.

From this connection, now open up to make contact with your Self. Do not ask any questions; it happens automatically when you are in a balanced state. Invite your Self to flow even more clearly throughout your body via the figure eight. Do not try too hard: it works better when you are in a receptive state. That is, when you do nothing actively, but instead let everything happen spontaneously.

Just be curious about what you feel, what you experience and what images arise.

What are the qualities of your Self? (Expect symbolic answers here that you may not understand in the first instance, but nevertheless receive them).

When you feel that you have achieved good contact with the Self, ask the following questions and wait for an answer each time:

What is my life's mission? Maybe you get an image, a metaphor or you hear a sound or get a certain feeling. Be very alert. The answer will be more of an abstract one, not very concrete yet. A practical answer will come later; allow yourself to record what comes in now without understanding it through your logic.

Then ask yourself the question: If this is my life's mission, who am I? Again, you usually receive an abstract answer.

Finish this exercise by taking a few more deep breaths in and out. Take a moment to write down your experiences afterwards.
 » The Self's qualities
 » My life mission
 » Who am I then?

From all of the above, try to create a metaphor that encompasses your identity.
 » I am like...

Tip:
Connected breathing is an exercise you can do on your own. You can then omit connecting with the Self like in the exercise. When you do this breathing exercise regularly, a balanced state naturally arises in which there is a connection with your three dynamics at the same time.

'Knowing others is intelligence;
knowing yourself is true wisdom.
Mastering others is strength;
mastering yourself is true power.'

– LAO TE CHING

Co-creating through RIO integration in practice

Now that you have good contact with your Self and are able to balance your three centers of intelligence, it is time to interact with the client in a renewed way. A comprehensive RIO salesperson uses I-HUC, a sequence of four repeating and deepening phases that take place in the sales process.

I-HUC is a spiral-shaped process that intensifies conversations through the energetic connection between yourself and your client. This connection enables the openness and vulnerability in which co-creation arises.

The circle in this drawing could somehow be represented as a spiral.

1 **I**nner balance
2 **H**eart-to-heart connection
3 **U**tter
4 **C**o-create

Let's take a closer look at each stage of the I-HUC process.

INNER BALANCE

Balancing your inner self through connected breathing should be a fixed morning ritual for every salesperson. An inner shower that you take every day, just like your physical shower. Because of this regularity, you are in better contact with yourself during the day and you automatically detect disturbances in your energy, also when you are in contact with others.

Before any form of contact with your customer – face to face, e-mail, telephone, etc. – consciously reconnect with your RIO channels (head – heart – abdomen) and balance them through your breathing technique. Two minutes of breathing is often enough, especially when you consciously balance your centers every day. Conscious breathing is then a reminder for your system, a wake-up call for each dynamic and an invitation to 'play along' in what follows.

Sometimes you will find it challenging to achieve balance. Certain thoughts keep going through your head, a remark from a client or colleague is not sitting well. You are not always able to do something about it on the spot. At these times you can only accept it for what it is. Try not to force anything or push yourself through mental strength, a battle you will lose anyway. In fact, you will often make the imbalance worse that way. Thanks to the inner scan and by accepting what is happening, you enter into contact with yourself and with the client, perhaps not fully balanced, but connected to your three channels of trust. During the conversation, continue to monitor what is going on within yourself and between you and the client.

Tip for when you notice a grating thought, twisted feeling or gnawing sensation within yourself:

Write down very briefly the physical sensations, images, emotions and thoughts you sensed during the inner scan. Later on, you will turn to this information again to discover which event reacted violently with which of your channels and what you need in such a context to achieve balance. Use the tables to gain insight into which center over- or underreacted. Afterwards, the exercise 'interview with your three centers of intelligence' can help you find out what is going on. The interview questions are directed specifically to the situation that created the bad feeling or the disturbing thought. An essential question is then: what does each center need in order to achieve balance? In the meantime, you already know the answers will come through metaphors, symbols, bodily sensations, so be particularly alert to that. If you receive an answer such as 'safety', it is up to you to find out how you can provide the dynamic with safety. You will not succeed by just reasoning logically and listing all safe circumstances, rather by making an energetic connection with the feeling of safety. Gradually you will come to know your system better and you will be able to add what you need on the spot.

HEART-TO-HEART CONNECTION
After the inner connection, you will make sincere connections with your clients. The channel par excellence for doing so is the heart. Remember the core qualities of the heart: connection, affection, feeling, values and criteria. Through your heart channel, you are able to pay attention to the relationship with the client. In your imagination, picture a bridge of light running from

your heart to the client's heart. You can send heart energy via the light over the bridge. Think of openness, sincerity, affection, respect, love.

Depending on your client's profile, this heart bridge will easily reach the client or not. With outgoing and informative customers, you will often notice that the bridge never even makes it to the beginning of your meetings. That is not a problem at all; do not force anything here but keep actively making the connection yourself. By doing so consciously, you tacitly invite the customer to appeal to the relational channel.

'Love, compassion and tolerance are not luxuries,

but necessities of life.'

– DALAI LAMA

UTTER

When starting with I-HUC, the most exciting phase is 'uttering' because you are naming what is going on between you and the customer and that is something vulnerable. In this step you are to express the following components:
- » What's going on inside of you.
- » What you see and feel with the customer.
- » Your (RIO) dynamics and especially their compatibility or pitfalls.

- **Saying what is going on inside you**

When expressing what is inside of you, you should always do it in the 'I' form, never in the 'you'. Feel the difference between 'I'm a bit restless because I would like to have more information', and 'You're not giving me enough information, so I'm restless.' The 'you'-form identifies a guilty party as the reason for your feelings. That is not true! The other is just a trigger for something that happens within you, not the cause of it. In his book *The Seven Habits of Highly Effective People*, Stephen Covey calls it the difference between being proactive and reactive. As a comprehensive RIO salesperson, you take responsibility for your own inner experience and name it in the 'I' form.

A few examples:
- » 'Because of my drive and enthusiasm, I tend to move forward quickly.'
- » 'I ask a lot of questions because I want to truly understand what you're looking for.'
- » 'I feel that that situation moves me.'

- **Expressing what you see and feel with the customer**

Naming what you see and feel with the customer is something you do in question form. In this way, you avoid establishing your observations as fact, and instead open up the possibility of a dialogue. If you state it as an established fact, then you are guaranteed a discussion about what you just said and that is not what you want to achieve. Notice the difference between: 'I am rather overwhelming to you; I feel that you're creating distance in the conversation' and 'Is it true that I seem rather overwhelming? There seems to be more distance between us in the conversation, do you feel that too?'

A few examples:
- » 'Do I sense that it's okay to go deeper into the technical information about our product?'
- » 'Could it be that we haven't yet reached the essence of what you're looking for?'
- » 'Am I correct in saying that it's better that I first explain the core of this application and go into details later, if necessary?'

- **Expressing the (RIO) dynamics**

By naming the RIO dynamics you get even more openness in a conversation. You indicate the complementarity of each interlocutor and appreciate everyone's strength. In addition, you let the client know that your style and approach are also an added value for them. You dance the RIO tango together in a very conscious, respectful and passionate way. If you and the client share the same RIO sequence, name it so that any gaps might come to the surface. Once the underexposed channel (R, I, O) becomes clear, you can search for a way to bring this missing dynamic into the collaboration.

A few examples:
- » 'Your hands-on approach and my attention to detail form a strong duo in this story.'
- » 'Your sensitivity and my sense of purpose complement each other well.'
- » 'I notice that we're both focused on creating a good interaction; there is a danger that we don't name what really matters because we don't want to hurt each other. May I know what's really going on?'
- » 'We've already worked out a lot of information. Shall we shed some light on the practical side of things as well?'

CO-CREATE

The co-creation phase is a natural continuation of all the previous steps. Here, you should make sure that you involve all of the centers in the creation process in a specific order. If not, there is a danger of slipping into creation based on your own preferred channels and that is a missed opportunity.

The specific order for (co-)creation:[12]

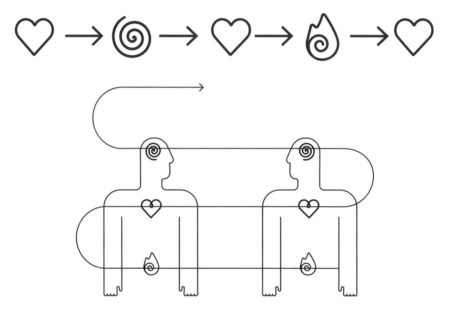

This order shows us very explicitly the leading role of the heart. It is through the relational channel of trust that we are able to connect with the greater whole, with our passion and our values. When in contact with our heart, our creations are by definition sustainable. As the seat of universal values and standards, your heart will not allow you to sell harmful products. You focus your attention on what adds value. You are also sincere in the situations where you cannot help the customer. The value of co-creation is truly looking for what the customer needs and looking more broadly at the role you can play in this.

Then you use your head dynamic to focus your creative thinking on the question. The head is a master in finding possibilities and solutions. Just consider the technical developments of the last two hundred years, the period in which we have fully developed our cognitive ability. However, over the past centuries we have been so focused on logic that we have forgotten to connect it with our hearts. Today our creations are fantastic advances in the direction of prosperity, but they are exhausting the system. We need to challenge our head dynamic much more to create based on a connection with the whole. Prosperity and sustainability can go hand in hand.

Let's return to the situation where your product does not fully meet the customer's needs.

Allow your creativity to go wild in this scenario. Maybe you put the customer in contact with someone in your network or maybe you need to add something new to your range. There are many possible solutions that go beyond the standard process. This is how it goes in a co-creative collaboration. With the various possibilities you then return to your heart dynamic and acquire valuable information with which, if necessary, you can make adjustments to the solutions you have come up with. The moment you and your client choose to implement one of the options, the abdominal dynamic comes into action. The abdominal dynamic's qualities are motivation, will, movement and courage. It often takes courage to do what the heart asks. Notice that when implementing your plan, you always return to the heart dynamic. The latter keeps its finger on the pulse.

Imagine you and your client using each of your three channels in this way in order to arrive at the best solution. Can you feel how this lends a deeper dimension to the salesperson's profession?

'Invention is not the product of logical thought,

even though the final product is tied to a logical structure.'

— ALBERT EINSTEIN

A beautiful illustration of I-HUC is the following true story from Jozefien:

> During a meeting with a client it was the intention to design a one-day training session together. The meeting started with identifying the needs that I, as an 'expert', would be able to address. As a consultant, I felt that more was needed than a one-day training session, but I doubted whether the participants would be open to the deeper work that RIO integration requires.

In other words, I was afraid that my proposal would be dismissed, afraid of being rejected.

A highly intuitive lady in the company recognized very well that the conversation, although objectively 'good', was not quite flowing. She said: 'I feel like we're dancing around something.' Because she expressed what she felt, the space and opening arose to deepen the conversation. Her instigation gave me the courage to name what I was struggling with. From a place of sincerity and vulnerability, I explained how I actually saw the process. A year-long course of action in which we would deep dive together and create movement within the entire organization. My proposal was warmly welcomed because everyone at the table felt that it was not about me or the training, but about the bigger picture. The valuable ideas and insights then followed spontaneously. We also got to know each other on a personal level, which ensured that we ended the conversation with an incredible sense of satisfaction and enthusiasm. Head, heart and belly on one line.

Let's have a look at the I-HUC process in this example.

Through continuous inner monitoring (I), Jozefien is very aware of the hesitation in her system to open up the conversation. She knows the underlying fear of rejection thanks to her prior inner work. Feeling so clearly while in conversation is only possible when you know your own system well and are self-aware in life.

The presence of the heart-to-heart connection (H) provided the opening to express (U) what was felt. Here it was the client who first named what she felt ('I feel like we're dancing around something'). With a good heart-to-heart connection all those involved become attuned to each other, so that 'uttering' has a cushion. It is not who expresses something that is important; what counts is that it happens. Thanks to the opening, Jozefien could gather the courage (I) to be vulnerable. Where is the vulnerability?

» For many, RIO integration is still a long way from their own reality. It is new and therefore not a mainstream story. Moreover, RIO integration asks every participant to open up and look at themselves. In a work environment this is not very commonplace.

» Furthermore, RIO integration is not just a day's worth of training, which the client might initially ask for, but an entire course of action. From a logical perspective, the chance that it will be rejected is reasonably high.

Co-creation (C) started spontaneously once all this had been said. Notice that co-creation starts from the heart. The value that resonated with each person present was the connection to the greater whole. It is around this value that a course of action is then built up and the most appropriate form and content are created.

'Knowledge coupled with a warm heart brings wisdom.'
— DALAI LAMA

A final word

This book is about how people can use their full potential in a profession with the ability to make a difference. How is that, you wonder? By creating a global movement.

Trade is one of the oldest professions in the world. A survey by LinkedIn shows that there are 21 million salespeople active today. What would it be like if these people all radiated love, wisdom and truthfulness in their many daily interactions?

What would it be like if we – entrepreneurs, businessmen and sales professionals – created and sold without trauma, regardless of the injuries we might have suffered in the past and that drive us toward power, money and prestige to compensate for our injured egos? What would it be like if we could make full use of our clear thinking, feeling, and actions, which are available at all times, if we just took the time to connect with them?

It is our conviction that it is not yet too late to start feeling, on an enormous scale, where the pain is that requires healing and to come up with a clear plan of action and begin to work fearlessly.

The products, technology and machines that will turn the tide must be produced and sold, preferably better and faster than those that are now polluting and exhausting the planet.

We hope that the knowledge contained in this book inspires people to find their way back to themselves. In doing so, we will also find our way back to each other and make a difference together.

#weareRIO

Endnotes

———

1   www.gartner.com
2   mBraining
3   Personal adaptation of a quote found on https://www.quora.com/What-is-the-essence-of-Buddhism-in-one-sentence
4   www.textgain.com
5   www.traicie.com
6   Ben Verhoeven TwiSty Paper, Reddit 'a gold mine for personality prediction' e.a.
7   www.erinmeyer.com
8   *Voice dialogue* from Hall and Sidra Stone
9   *mBraining*
10 Psychoenergetics refers to a set of knowledge, insights, values and skills regarding the optimal performance of the human *psyche* (principle of life, soul, source, being), considered in its most integral and multidimensional aspects. In other words, psychoenergetics delves into the multidimensional and subtle energy-related aspects of human communication, behavior and consciousness – www.timotheus.org.
11 Reference to Schrödinger's quantum mechanics thought experiment.
12 mBraining